CITIES IN NEW TESTAMENT TIMES

Charles Ludwig

ACCENT BOOKS

"Accustomed to superhighways, air and space travel, we smugly assume that communications during the lives of the apostles were perhaps even more primitive than they were in colonial America. This is a mistake. Paul and other New Testament workers had easy access to an amazing network of all-weather roads that were unexcelled until half a century ago..." Charles Ludwig's edge-of-the-seat stories make twelve first-century cities vibrate anew with life. You will find yourself walking down these roads with Paul as he carries the gospel to other cities.

CITIES
IN NEW TESTAMENT TIMES
Charles Ludwig

CITIES
IN NEW TESTAMENT TIMES

Charles Ludwig

ACCENT BOOKS
Denver, Colorado

MEMBER OF
EVANGELICAL CHRISTIAN
PUBLISHERS ASSOCIATION

All rights reserved. No portion of this book may be reproduced in any form without the written permission of the publishers, with the exception of brief excerpts in magazine reviews.

Accent Publications
12100 W. Sixth Avenue
P.O. Box 15337
Denver, Colorado 80215

Copyright © 1976 B/P Publications, Inc.
Printed in U.S.A.

Library of Congress Catalog Card Number: 75-41480
ISBN 0-916406-16-4

Preface

The New Testament is the greatest book ever written. But even in modern translations, many find it dull. Why? Largely because it is difficult for them to identify with what is written.

To many, such places as Tarsus, Ephesus, and Antioch are just vague names with no real meaning. But if such people, as they read the epistles, could visualize an eager messenger carrying them along the Via Egnatia; or if they could see Dleopatra, dressed like Aphrodite, sailing up the Cydnus to Tarsus, those epistles would suddenly leap into life and demand to be read.

Or what about Ephesus? Is it a living, thriving place? To many it is not. But to those who know about its huge temple, its edge-of-the-seat history, and its determined silversmiths, it comes alive, and causes the book of Ephesians to quiver with life.

This book deals with the story of a dozen cities. Its purpose is to give a brief history of these cities, and to help them to become real to each reader.

Like our previous book, *Rulers of New Testament Times*, this book is not for the technical scholar. Rather, it is for the serious Bible student, the Sunday School teacher, the preacher without a vast library—and for those interested in a good story.

If from this book you can find a few hours of reading pleasure, or a window to illuminate a lesson or a talk, it will be worth my effort.

Charles Ludwig
Tucson, Arizona

For Wade B. Jakeway

Illustrations

Wheel of a Roman chariot found in Pompeii 11
Charles Ludwig photo
Ancient inn on Appian Way outside Rome 16
Charles Ludwig photo
Entrance to Domitta Catacomb near Rome 19
Courtesy of Pont. Comm. Di Arch.
Mamertine Prison where Paul was held in Rome 21
Charles Ludwig photo
Remains of the old Roman Forum near Mamertine Prison 22
Courtesy Trans World Airlines
The Parthenon in Athens 33
Charles Ludwig photo
The approach to Mars' Hill 37
Charles Ludwig photo
The canal crossing the Isthmus of Corinth 41
Charles Ludwig photo
The Lechaion Road in Corinth 44
Charles Ludwig photo
The Acrocorinth near ancient Corinth 45
Charles Ludwig photo
Interior of jail at Philippi where Paul and Silas were miraculously released. Inscription quotes Philippians 1:21 in Greek and English 49
Charles Ludwig photo

The Angites River (above) where Lydia was baptized and Hotel Lydia today nearby   55
Charles Ludwig photo

Present seaport at Thessalonica (Salonica)   61
Charles Ludwig photo

New Thessalonica built around the ancient city   62
Charles Ludwig photo

An artist's idea of the Temple of Artemis (Diana)   67
Charles Ludwig photo

Antioch from across the Orontes River, from a woodcut by Louis Cassas who visited the city in 1787   77
Charles Ludwig photo

The Cilician Gates, a historical pass near Tarsus   85
V. Pearson photo

An oasis near Jericho   91
Courtesy Israeli Tourist Office

Jericho, city of palms, history and sorrow   92
Charles Ludwig photo

An agricultural station in Jericho   95
Charles Ludwig photo

"O Little Town of Bethlehem"   99
Courtesy Israeli Tourist Office

Nativity Square in Bethlehem   100
Charles Ludwig photo

Silver star in marble floor marks where Jesus was born in a stable   104
Charles Ludwig photo

The Damascus Gate, Jerusalem   107
Israeli Tourist Office

Gordon's Calvary—the place of a skull   109
Charles Ludwig photo

The Garden Tomb   112
Charles Ludwig photo

Mary's Well in Nazareth   119
Courtesy of Israeli Tourist Office

A street scene in Nazareth   122
Courtesy Israeli Tourist Office

A shop for tourists in Nazareth   124
Charles Ludwig photo

Contents

Chapter 1. Communications **11**

Chapter 2. Rome **19**

Chapter 3. Athens **33**

Chapter 4. Corinth **41**

Chapter 5. Philippi **49**

Chapter 6. Thessalonica **61**

Chapter 7. Ephesus **67**

Chapter 8. Antioch **77**

Chapter 9. Tarsus **85**

Chapter 10. Jericho **91**

Chapter 11. Bethlehem **99**

Chapter 12. Jerusalem **107**

Chapter 13. Nazareth **119**

Bibliography **127**

CHAPTER 1

Communications

In order to understand these intriguing cities of the New Testament era, we must first understand how they received their supplies and how they communicated with one another.

Accustomed to superhighways, air and space travel, we smugly assume that communications during the lives of the apostles were perhaps even more primitive than they were in colonial America. This is a mistake. Paul and other New Testament workers had easy access to an amazing network of all-weather roads that were unexcelled until half a centry ago.

When King William IV appointed Sir Robert Peel prime minister in 1834, Peel was enjoying the sunshine of Rome. Upon receiving the word, Peel—founder of the London police—spared no expense to get to London as soon as possible. The journey took 30 days—a day longer than was required by Caesar's postal system in 54 B.C.

At the death of Augustus Caesar (A.D. 14), the Roman Empire contained 3,340,000 square miles. This means it was slightly larger than the continental United States. And living within this area was a population, estimated

Communications

by Gibbon, of 120,000,000. To maintain the *Pax Romana*—Roman Peace—it was necessary to be able to move troops and supplies quickly. Thus, good highways throughout the Empire were a number one priority.

In Italy alone there were 372 main routes and 12,000 miles of paved highways. And altogether, throughout the Empire, there were 51,000 miles of paved roads in addition to a large network of secondary thoroughfares. One of these paved roads stretched from Jerusalem to Boulogne!

With such a maze of roads, maps were necessary. These "itineraries" indicated the routes, the distances, and even some of the views along the way. There were even travel books. Will Durant in his *Caesar and Christ,* declared flatly, "Despite all difficulties, there was probably more traveling in Nero's day than at any time before our birth."

Unlike even our best superhighways, Roman roads were built to last centuries. The various Latin names for the ingredients they used have worked their way into English. The bottom layer of a road was made from a four- to six-inch layer of tightly packed sand known as *pavimentum.* On top of this were placed four layers of other materials.

The first of these was the *statumen*—a foot-thick flow of small stones mixed with clay or cement. This was covered with ten inches of rammed concrete known as the *rudens.* Then over this was spread the *nucleus* made up of rolled concrete from 12 to 18 inches thick. This was then topped with the *summa crusta* made of slabs of lava or silex from eight inches to a foot thick so skillfully joined that the separations were scarsely visible.

Usually the center of the road was higher than the edges, thus providing drainage. A normal highway was 16 to 24 feet wide. For chariots, pack animals, and pedestrians it was fully adequate. As the roads neared a city, part of this width was absorbed by *margines*—sidewalks.

Roman roads were generally straight. This means that they had to cross rivers, marshes, mountains. Frequently their engineers made tunnels, even through mountains of

Communications

rock. When a road sided a mountain, it was buttressed from beneath with burned brick, stone, and mortar.

Their bridges were excellent and were made to last. From the Egyptians they had learned some of the secrets of hydraulic engineering. When a peer was to be made, they drove double cylinders down through the water and deep into the soil. Both cylinders were made watertight, and the water was pumped out from between them. The space between the cylinders was then filled with cement. Using this method, eight magnificent bridges were built across the Tiber. Some of these are still in use!

Along the highways, a marker was laid down every mile to indicate the distance to the next town. Every ten miles there was a *statio* where one could hire fresh horses. In addition, a *mansio* was erected at every 30-mile interval. At these inns, one could buy supplies and even spend the night. Luke was referring to such a place when he wrote: "When the brethren heard of us, they came to meet us as far as Appii forum, and The three taverns: whom when Paul saw, he thanked God, and took courage" (Acts 28:15).

Mansios had a reputation for immorality, high prices, and even robbery. Wise travelers continued on to the *civities*—cities—where they could secure rooms in safer and more moderately priced hotels.

These highways cost about $10,000 per mile to build. But considering their durability, this was a bargain price. In New Testament times, the entire tax income from the Empire was about $150,000,000. These estimates were made by Will Durant who was thinking in terms of 1940 dollars. In our time this is less than the tax income of many a moderate-sized American city. But the Caesars did not flinch to spend money on roads.

Realizing that the Romans did not have explosives or heavy modern equipment, people today question how the roads were built. The answer is that they had pulleys, cranes, vertical beams, windlasses, huge treadmills operated by men and animals, and slaves—millions of slaves. Moreover, the Romans were excellent mathe-

Communications

maticians.

Normally a chariot could average 40 or 50 miles a day on these roads. But in an emergency they could move faster. At the time of Nero's suicide, a messenger got the news to Galba in Spain, 332 miles away, in 36 hours. Undoubtedly the record, however, was set by Tiberius. He traveled 600 miles in three days to get to the bedside of his dying brother. To manage this, he used relays of chariots.

For those who could afford it, there was an even more pleasant way to travel. This was by the use of the *carruca*—or better yet, the *carruca dormitoria*. This was an ancient sedan chair which was carried by a quartet of men, each with the end of a supporting pole on his shoulder. The carruca dormitoria was complete with beds, and for a price one could go to sleep and wake up in another town 50 miles away. Cicero relates that he once met a man equipped with "two chariots, a carriage, a litter, horses, numerous slaves, and besides a monkey on a little car, and a number of wild asses."

Traveling throughout the Roman Empire had several advantages over crossing the same area today. No passports were needed. Roman money could be used anywhere. Likewise, they had some modern conveniences. Letters of credit were available and so were traveler's checks.

A one percent sales tax was levied on tourists and traders. There were no highway patrolmen and no one was arrested for speeding or crossing a yellow line. But soldiers were frequently stationed along the more dangerous routes because of the danger of highwaymen.

One of the Roman highways is especially famous today because it was used by Paul. Following their conquest of the Balkan Peninsula, the Romans had need of a highway to stretch out far into the east. And so the famous Egnatian Way was constructed. Reaching from Dyrrhachium on the west coast of Macedonia, it threaded its way across the Balkans, Thessalonica, Amphipolis, Philippi, and on to Byzantium—modern Istanbul.

Communications

The route followed by this road was a famous one. It had been used by Xerxes, Darius, and Alexander the Great. Portions of this road are still in existence and a number of the original milestones have been discovered.

The Romans did not have a zip code, nor a mail box on the corner. Their empire flourished and died long before the first postage stamp was issued in 1840. But the Caesars did have systems with which to communicate, and some of them were fairly rapid.

When the grain bins in the capital were nearly empty, semaphore signals from Puteoli—one hundred and fifty miles south of Rome—flashed the vital news that grain-laden ships were on their way. This type of signalling was done by relays from one high point to another. The Romans also used carrier pigeons.

Mainly, however, the government depended on the firmly established *cursus publicus*—postal system. This organization was perfected by Augustus Caesar, the emperor who was ruling when Jesus was born. The heart of the system was the use of innumerable relays of horses that were stabled every few miles. The port of Neapolis through which Paul and his companions made entrance into Europe after the Macedonian call, is now named Kavalla. Kavalla is vulgar Latin for horse, and the port received this name because it was one of the terminals in the Roman postal system.

Each stable along the way was supposed to keep approximately forty horses. With so many mounts available, a letter could be moved 100 miles a day. In times of emergency, of course, this speed could be exceeded. The carrier—often a slave—was known as the *tabellarius*. For a badge, he wore a small bronze shield.

Our English word post comes from the Latin *positus* which means placed. It referred to the way horses were placed at certain intervals along the Roman roads.

The Romans had the greatest and most successful postal system of antiquity. But they were not the originators. The motto on the New York City Post Office:

Communications

An inn, which also served as a relay station for horses that carried the mail, stood at every thirty miles on all major Roman roads. This inn still stands on the Appian Way just outside Rome.

Communications

"Neither snow nor rain nor heat nor gloom of night stay these couriers from the swift completion of their rounds" was written by Herodotus. This Greek historian—484-425 B.C.—was referring to a system originated by the Persians!

The Persian king Cyrus—600-529 B.C.—is said to have invented the relay system. It was he who tested the endurance of a horse and determined how far apart they should be spaced.

In the book of Esther—dated by conservative scholars from 485 to 465 B.C.—we read: "And he [Mordecai] wrote in the king Ahasuerus' name, and sealed it with the king's ring, and sent letters by posts on horseback, and riders on mules, camels, and young dromedaries" (Esther 8:10). But long before the appearance of Cyrus, we have the record in Job which says: "Now my days are swifter than a post" (Job 9:25).

But as swift as the Roman post was, it was used almost exclusively for the government. Only on rare occasions could private citizens send mail by the *cursus publicus*, and when this privilege was permitted they had to have an official *diploma*—double-fold—with the right seals and signatures. The normal private citizen sent his mail by a slave, a tourist, or a special friend.

The apostles, of course, used the Roman roads for much of their travel and correspondence. But they also made use of the sea-lanes. Although Roman ships were driven by sails, some were quite large and could average about six knots per hour. If this seems slow, remember that the Mayflower only averaged two miles per hour!

Many of the ships could carry as many as 600 passengers along with several thousand tons of freight. Passage was cheap. The fare from Athens to Alexandria was less than two American dollars. However, this was for deck passengers, and they were required to provide their own food.

The distance covered by ships in those days is amazing. All of the Mediterranean ports could be reached. In

Communications

addition, ships went regularly to other parts of the world. In A.D. 80 a book appeared to guide captains to the east coast of Africa and to India. Thirty years before the appearance of this book, Hippalus had charted the frequency and direction of the monsoon winds. And through this discovery, he was able to sail directly from Aden across the ocean to India in about forty days. These charts made him as famous in his day as Columbus is in ours.

But as efficient as the Roman ships were, they were not always available—nor reliable. The compass had not been discovered. There were many wrecks and many pirates. To combat the pirates, Augustus stationed two war fleets near the coasts of Italy. One was at Ravenna on the Adriatic and the other on the opposite side of the Italian boot at Naples. Still, piracy was always a threat. Julius Caesar was especially aware of this, for he was once captured by pirates and held for ranson.

The main threat to shipping, however, was the weather. Few captains were willing to sail between November and March. This was because the cold winters made sailing dangerous. It was because of this hazard that Paul wrote to Timothy: "Do thy diligence to come shortly unto me.... Only Luke is is with me. Take Mark, and bring him with thee: for he is profitable to me for the ministry.... *Do thy dilligence to come before winter*" (II Timothy 4:9,11,21).

Another peril to Roman shipping were the periodic typhoons. And any reader of the travels of Paul knows how dangerous these winds could be.

Altogether, Paul was shipwrecked four times. (In II Corinthians 11:25, Paul remarked that he had been shipwrecked three times; and so his shipwreck near Malta on his way to a Roman prison was his fourth.) But in spite of all the obstacles to effective communications, transportation and the dissemination of information throughout the Empire was amazingly reliable. By the time of Diocletian toward the end of the third century, the postal system was opened to the entire public. Indeed, the mails became so heavy, Diocletian frequently punished Christians by forcing them to carry mail!

CHAPTER 2

Rome

The Rome in which Paul was imprisoned was not only the ruling hub of the entire Mediterranean world, it was also the busiest and by far the most interesting city on earth.

Overflowing with luxury, history, and magnificent buildings, it was called the Eternal City. Likewise, knowing of the vice and corruption that lingered along its avenues, and between its more than three hundred public fountains, some—and with good reason—dubbed it The Sewer of the Empire. The Rome in which Paul was chained contained both extremes. But before we start peering and sniffing down its streets, let's see how the great apostle got there. For after all, the letters that Paul wrote and his execution just south of the city, are the most far-reaching contributions to the fame of this metropolis on the Tiber.

Having appealed to Caesar, Paul was fettered to other prisoners and sent to Rome for trial. Surviving a terrible shipwreck, he finally landed at Puteoli. There, by permission of Julius, the Roman officer in charge of the prisoners, Paul remained with friends for a week. Then he proceeded to Rome on foot.

Rome

At the market of Appius, forty-three miles south of the capital on the Appian Way, he was met by a delegation of Christians who had made the two-day journey in order to greet him and make him feel welcome in the midst of anxiety. Ten miles further up at an inn called Three Taverns, he was greeted by yet another delegation. Here, as Luke recorded, "he thanked God, and took courage" (Acts 28:15).

It is unknown who organized these welcoming parties, but it has been surmised that it was Epaphroditus—the one who had been sent to Paul with a gift from the church at Philippi. Also, one questions why these Roman Christians were so enthusiastic about Paul. A logical reason is that they had been exposed to the book of Romans which Paul had written in Corinth in A.D. 55 or 56—five or six years before his arrival in Italy.

Paul, along with the other prisoners, entered Rome through the Porta Capena. Today this place cannot be precisely identified. But we do know that it was the very beginning of the Appian Way. At the time, a 350-year-old aqueduct—Aqua Appia—passed overhead.

The Appian Way was named after Appius Claudius, the man who started it in 312 B.C. In his later years he was dubbed Appius Claudius Caecus "the Blind." Legend has it that he was so proud of his accomplishment the gods struck him blind. This magnificent highway was used without interruption for over one thousand years.

It has been surmised that Paul's guard Julius was a member of the Praetorian Guard. If this was the case, Paul was probably taken immediately to the Praetorian headquarters on the *Palatine Hill* in almost the heart of Rome. There are some who claim, however, that Julius was a special messenger and a member of the Peregrini. If this is so, Paul would have been led to the Peregrini camp on the *Caelian Hill* to the right.

The rank or order of Julius is unimportant. But to get a general idea of ancient or modern Rome it is necessary to understand that it was compressed onto seven low, flat-

Rome

The Mamertine Prison where Paul was imprisoned is near the Roman Forum. The tiny dungeon was cold and miserable (ritual worship and modern tourist items have been added); nevertheless, Paul wrote some of his immortal epistles from this place.

Rome

As the modern visitor climbs the steps out of the Mamertine Prison, he may cross a modern paved street and look down upon the ancient pavement and remains of the old Roman Forum.

Rome

topped hills bordered on the west by the gently curving Tiber.

The Romans then, as now, thought in terms of these hills.

At the time of Paul's imprisonment, Rome was considered to be over 800 years old. Those who accepted the idea that the city was founded by Romulus and Remus—the twins who were nursed by a wolf—believed that it dated back to 753 B.C.

The city Paul faced had a population of approximately one million. Half of these were slaves. The total circumference was about twelve miles.

Having been delivered by Julius "to the captain of the guard," Paul was given the privilege of remaining with a soldier "in his own hired house." Perhaps this special favor was arranged by Julius who had learned to appreciate and trust Paul during their perilous journey.

Rentals in Rome, even in the poorest section, were expensive. Born in Rome in 60 or 61—the approximate time of Paul's arrival—Juvenal knew the city extremely well. To a friend he wrote: "If you can tear yourself away from the games of the Circus, you can buy an excellent house at Sora . . . for what you now pay in Rome to rent a dark garret for one year."

Remembering that Paul once reminded the Corinthians "We both hunger, and thirst, and are naked, and are buffeted, and have no certain dwelling place" (I Corinthians 4:11), we wonder how he could afford even the shabbiest rental—especially with legal fees to pay. The answer is, that the gift brought by Epaphroditus was probably a generous one. It is not difficult to imagine that before he started out on his 850-mile trip to Rome, he said to the Philippians, "Now let's be liberal. Prices here are high, but they are much higher in Rome."

Since Rome had only a tiny middle class, the Romans were unusually rich or desperately poor. The rich built elaborate houses equipped with fine swimming pools and special gardens. Few were higher than two stories. Cellars

Rome

were practically unknown. Some houses had central heating, but in most the heat was distributed by portable charcoal braziers.

Floors were of concrete or tile. Many had mosaics worked into them. The plumbing was of lead—long sheets were hammered around a slender piece of steel to form a pipe. Expensive statues occupied honored positions and lovely paintings decorated the walls. In addition, most houses boasted of at least one fountain and rain water was drained from the roof by lead gutters.

The rich lived in luxury.

Even though Luke tells us that Paul "dwelt two whole years in his own hired house, and received all that came in unto him" (Acts 28:30), it is unlikely that he lived in an expensive place. Most scholars are agreed that Paul's room or suite of rooms was undoubtedly in one of Rome's large tenement buildings. These block-sized structures were so enormous they were called *insulae*—islands. Since the working classes lived in these apartment houses, and since there was no public transportation, most of the *insulae* were toward the center of the city. This was so the workers could be near their places of employment.

Augustus had decreed that a front of a building could never be more than seventy feet high. But apparently the builders found a loophole in the law and made the back parts higher than the front. Living in Rome in 64, Martial wrote about "a poor devil whose attic is 200 steps up." Shops and offices occupied the ground floor just as they do in modern hotels.

Without street lighting, the areas around an *insula* could be dangerous. Juvenal commented: "And now regard the different and diverse perils of the night. See what a height it is to that towering roof from which a potsherd comes crack on my head every time that broken or leaky vessel is pitched out a window! See with what a smash it strikes and dints the pavement! There's death in every open window as you pass along at night; you may well be deemed a fool, improvident of sudden accident, if

Rome

you go out to dinner without having made your will. You can but hope, and put up a piteous prayer in your heart, that they may be content to pour down on your head the contents of their slop-pails."

Unless Epaphroditus had been fortunate in meeting a friend of Paul's when he entered the city, he would have had a most difficult time in finding him. This is because the Romans did not number their houses, and secondary streets did not have names! An ancient comedy of Roman times has survived. The play shows how difficult it was to find an address in Rome. The following exchange is between the slave Syrus and the elderly Demea:

Syrus. Well, I can't recall the name of the man he's gone to see, but I know where he lives.

Demea. Well, tell me the place.

Syrus. Down this way. You know the porch beside the butcher's?

Demea. Yes, of course.

Syrus. Pass this way straight up the street, and when you have gone so far, there's a slope in front of you; go down, and after that there lies a little chapel with an alley close by.

Demea. Where do you mean?

Syrus. Where the big wild fig-tree grows.

Demea. I know.

Syrus. Yes, of course. Heavens! What a fool I am! You must come back again to the porch. Yes, that's also far quicker and less roundabout. Do you know where the wealthy Cratinus lives?

Demea. I do.

Syrus. Well, pass his house, then go left straight down this street, and turn right at Diana's shrine. Before you reach the city gate, just near the pool, there's a bakery with a carpenter's shop opposite. He's there.

Quoted in *Rome Its People Life and Customs* by Ugo Paoli.

Rome

But even if one knew exactly where to go in Rome, he might still face hazards on the way. Juvenal tells us what it was like. "Most sick people here in Rome perish for want of sleep, the illness itself having been produced by food lying undigested on a fevered stomach. For what sleep is possible in a lodging? Who but the wealthy ever get sleep in Rome? There lies the root of the disorder. The crossing of wagons in the narrow winding streets, the slanging of drovers when brought to a stand, would make sleep impossible for a Drusus [a Roman general famous for his strength]—or a sea-calf. When the rich man has a call of social duty, the mob makes way for him as he is born swiftly over their heads in a huge Liburnian car. He writes or sleeps as he goes along, for the closed window of the litter induces slumber. Yet he will arrive before us; hurry as we may, we are blocked by a surging crowd in front, and by a dense mass of people pressing in on us from behind: one man digs an elbow into me, another a sedan-pole; one bangs a beam, another a wine-cask against my head. My legs are besplattered with mud; huge feet trample on me from every side, and a soldier plants his hobnails firmly on my toe."

Most Romans who went out at night had a slave precede them with a lantern.

Yes, Rome had a vast sewage system and some of it is still in use. But it was not as efficient as one might suppose. In the days of Paul, one of the main arteries of this network was the *Cloaca Maxima*. Unfortunately this huge drain which was started hundreds of years before Christ, carried rain water as well as sewage. Even worse, it emptied into the Tiber!

Because these mammoth drains carried storm water, long widemouthed openings had to be made into the streets. The result was that Rome was frequently heavy with the stench of sewage.

An early discovery that had revolutionized Rome was cement. *Caementicum,* made by mixing volcanic ash with bits of brick, fragments of marble, and sand, was first

Rome

developed about 200 B.C. This cement was extremely hard and durable.

With it, engineers were equipped to build great buildings, roads, bridges, aqueducts. Altogether, Rome was supplied by fourteen aqueducts. Measuring a total of 1300 miles—the distance from New York City to Omaha, Nebraska—these stone and brick arteries plunged through mountains, across valleys, and over marshes. They delivered three hundred million gallons of water daily.

This seems like an overabundance of water. But the Romans needed it for their elaborate fountains, artificial lakes, vast public baths, and gardens. Moreover, almost every house had a bath tub, and the Romans bathed every day. But then, as now, there were those who connected secretly onto the water in order to avoid payment. This meant that a corps of inspectors had to be employed.

If Epaphroditus arrived in Rome in November, he would not have seen the effects of the almost annual floods. But if his arrival was in the spring, and if he came by sea, he would have shuddered at the devastation brought by the overflowing Tiber. Tacitus wrote: "Men were swept away by the waves or sucked under by the eddies; beasts of burden, baggage, lifeless bodies floated about and blocked their way."

The one-thousand-foot-long Emporium stood on the eastern side of the Tiber. Here, Epaphroditus could see—and smell—the vastness of the trade that flowed in and out of Rome. Crammed with little shops and eager merchants, one could hear chatter and haggling in a dozen languages. In some ways the Emporium resembled the Grand Bazaar in modern Istanbul.

Almost anything could be purchased in Rome. Geese were driven down the highways from far-off Belgium. This was to satisfy the keen demand for goose liver. From other parts of the world came silks, wine, gold, wheat, ivory. Without much searching, one could purchase honey, parchments, drugs, fruit, glass, perfumes, jewelry.

Rome

Usually slaves were sold at public auction; and since there was a constant demand, there were many auctions where they could be purchased. At a typical auction, the fettered slave mounted a platform and faced his bidders. A scroll which included a six-month guarantee was draped from the victim's neck. In this document, the name, nationality, skills, and character were listed. Also the person's health was carefully described. No one wanted to pay good money for an epileptic. Usually a doctor was on hand. This man would ask the slave to strip and then he would announce to potential buyers the slave's physical condition.

The price of slaves varied. Dealers often followed the Roman armies. After a victory, a spear was driven into the ground and a buyer began to make purchases. The generals liked this system. It saved them from the problem of dealing with prisoners of war.

As captives were brought to this place to be sold, a wreath was placed around each one's head which stated: *sub corona venire*—to be sold under the crown. The price on the battlefield was as low as $1. This was because it was understood that many of the slaves would die before they reached the markets of Rome. Unused to slavery, many prisoners of war committed suicide. An educated slave might bring a high price. This is because they could be used in the professions. But the price of a laborer was usually less than $100. Horace—65-68 B.C.—mentioned a slave who was purchased by Marcus Scaurus for $28,000.

At the auction, slaves without a guarantee wore caps and imported slaves had their feet whitened with chalk. One reason for this is that there was a special duty on imported slaves.

Shopping in Rome was like shopping in a modern city. At the time paper money was not in circulation. But there was a sales tax, and it had to be paid in cash.

If Epaphroditus happened to have stopped at a book stall, he would have seen descriptions and lists of titles pasted on the outside walls. Roman book stores were filled

Rome

with scrolls made of both parchment and papyrus. Also, they contained many codices—bound books. Books were published in editions of one thousand, and considering that they had to be copied by hand, the price was reasonable. Small volumes sold for about $1.50, while deluxe editions which often included the portrait of the author, brought around $3.

Libraries, both private and public, were popular. One of the better known of these, *Bibliotheca Ulpia,* was started by Trajan. Quite often there were reading rooms at the public baths. And, as in modern times, the better libraries often displayed the busts of notable citizens.

The Romans loved to eat—and drink. In just the city of Rome 25,000,000 gallons of wine were consumed annually. This works out to about two quarts per week for every man, woman, or child, slave or citizen.

The very rich spent much of their time eating. A typical banquet started at four in the afternoon and continued until late at night. The favorite meat was pork, and according to Pliny a pig could be served in at least fifty forms. A favorite dish—invented by Tiberius—was made from the liver of a pig fattened on figs. At such banquets the tables were decorated with flowers, the air was scented with perfume, and the servants were in crisp livery. Music was also provided, and beautiful women, often in the nude, or nearly so, were displayed.

Exotic foods of every imaginable type were served. Eels and snails were popular, and so were flamingo tongues, ostrich wings, and song birds.

After a Roman had stuffed himself until he couldn't swallow another bite, he simply excused himself and went to the *vomitorium.* Seneca complained at this practice. Said he, *"Vomunt ut edant, edant ut vomant*—they vomit to eat and eat to vomit." Having lost their food, they staggered back to the table to eat more.

All sorts of nationalities jostled one another in the streets. And one did not have to be an expert to sort them out. Most of the Romans were clean-shaven, that is until

Rome

the time of Hadrian. The down from a youth's first shave was generally dedicated to a god. The backward Britons were conspicuous because of their tattoos and uncouth ways.

Slaves were also easily discernible. Normally a slave wore a tunic and wooden shoes. Also, if he had tried to escape, the letter F, for *fugitivus,* was branded on his forehead. Others had metal collars riveted around their necks. Some of these collars have been preserved. One carries the inscription: *Fugi. Tene me. Cum Revocaveris me d.m. Zonino, accipis solidum*—"I have run away. Catch me. If you take me back to my master Zoninus you'll be rewarded."

The Jewish population was generally about 20,000, and they dressed much as they did in Jerusalem—full beards and all. Although frequently exiled from Rome, most of them usually returned when the emperor's wrath had cooled. On the whole, however, the Jews were not the business leaders of the time. The leading tradesmen were Syrians and Greeks.

The toga was worn only on formal occasions, and it was worn only by Roman citizens. The most distinguished foreigners were not allowed to wear it; and should a citizen be exiled, he was required to leave his toga in Italy.

For normal street wear, the Romans donned blouses. There were no buttons or stockings. Generally the men clipped their hair short. But there were some dandies who sported wigs, and an occasional baldy painted hair on his pate. Fashionable women used rouge, had numerous slaves spend several hours trimming their nails, curling their hair, and darkening their brows and lashes. Some bathed in donkey milk. Indeed, Poppaea—Nero's wife—was so obsessed with this idea, she had a herd of donkeys driven along wherever she traveled!

Since the Romans, until the time of Hadrian, cremated their dead, there were no Western-type cemeteries. And those Romans who did insist on burial were generally entombed by the side of the highways. This they were

Rome

allowed to do provided the monument was elaborate enough. Remains of such monuments may still be seen along the Appian Way.

Without cemeteries for their dead, the Jews dug underground passages outside the city and placed the bodies in crypts cut into the walls. The soft volcanic stone known as tufa was easily cut. In time, workers, known as fossores, specialized in doing this work. And thus the famous system of catacombs was born. Following the death of Paul, Christians began to make new catacombs. They used these tunnels for their dead, as hiding places, and sometimes extra large rooms were excavated in order to have large rooms where Christians could worship.

The combined length of the catacombs under modern Rome and its environs is estimated to be six hundred miles!

When strangers without funds died in Rome, their bodies were flung into twelve-foot square holes on the eastern side of Esquiline Hill. These graves also served for the disposal of dead animals. Since the pits were not covered, the stench was almost unbearable. This area was something like a city dump. Waste which could not be disposed through the regular sewer system was carted there. This hill was also the place where criminals were executed. When crucified, the victim was not removed from the cross. Instead, the body was left hanging for the birds, wolves, and other beasts of prey which thronged the area.

In his later days, Augustus boasted, "I found Rome built of sun-dried brick; I leave her clothed in marble." And to a large extent this was true. On his way to Paul's lodging, Epaphroditus undoubtedly saw marble on every side. There were long colonnades with tall marble columns, dazzling white public buildings, and many temples in honor of the gods. Suetonius noted that Augustus "restored ruined or burned temples, beautifying these and others with the most lavish gifts: for instance a single donation to Capitoline Jupiter of 16,000 pounds of gold,

Rome

besides pearls..." *(The Twelve Caesars by Seutonius)*. To achieve beauty, he did not spare money.

The Colosseum, however, did not exist in Paul's day. Before the time of that building, the throngs flocked to sports events at the Circus Maximus.

Traffic problems in Rome were not as acute as in our larger cities. Still, they had them, and were forced to take drastic action. Julius Caesar decreed:

> ... no one shall drive a wagon along the streets... in the suburbs where there is continuous housing after sunrise or before the tenth hour of the day, except whatever will be proper for the transportation... of material for building temples of the immortal gods, or for public works, or for removing from the city rubbish... (Quoted in *The Appian Way, A Journey* by Dora Jane Hamblin and Mary Jane Crunsfeld).

Whether or not the traffic moved on the right or the left is unknown. Albert C. Rose, however, has suggested that the side of the road "varied depending on where the driver was sitting in relation to his hitch and his carriage."

The Rome of New Testament times was an old and solid city. If during the time of Paul's incarceration, someone had suggested that the Roman Empire would fall, that person would have been considered insane. And yet it came to pass. In 410, Alaric and his Goths swept into Italy. They even captured Rome and looted it for three terrible days. And half a century later it was captured again and looted—this time by the Vandals.

Ironically, the final emperor of Rome was a lad named Romulus—the identical name of the mythical founder of the city!

This terrible drama inspired a Persian poet to write:

"The spider weaves the curtains in the palaces of the Caesars; the owl calls the watches of Afrasiab's towers."

CHAPTER 3

Athens

Paul frequently retreated. But his retreats were always advances. Hounded by a mob in one city, he simply moved to the next. One priority flamed through his life. This priority was to preach Jesus Christ—everywhere!

Because of the mobs, Paul finally headed toward Athens, the sparkling center of Greek culture. One can only imagine his surging feelings as he entered this city of white marble. Crowned by the Parthenon, already nearly five hundred years old, Athens was a symbol of progressive thought and a democratic spirit.

Coins with the image of Athena—the patron goddess of Athens—stamped on them had been a collector's item in Paul's boyhood city of Tarsus, for ever since the conquests of Alexander the Great, Greek power and ideas had been felt throughout the land of the Jews—and beyond.

Undoubtedly while Paul was studying in the various places of learning, books written by and about the various great men of Athens had come to his attention. One can visualize him as a school boy winding and unwinding the scrolls of Socrates, Plato, Aristotle, Euripides. Like most educated Jews, Paul spoke fluent Greek. He also probably

Athens

smiled at some of the older rabbis—especially in the more obscure places. In the past, some of them so hated the Greek language they were convinced it was just as sinful to speak Greek as it was to eat pork! This was in spite of the fact that the Old Testament had been translated into Greek hundreds of years before. The rabbis believed that Hebrew was the sacred tongue.

Paul, however, was most thankful for Greek, for it had become an international language that was understood in the entire Mediterranean world. Thus, with Greek at his disposal, and the use of the Roman all-weather roads, it was much easier to spread the Good News of Jesus Christ.

Like every scholar of his time, Paul knew something of the history of Athens. Around eleven hundred years before the birth of Jesus, the then tiny city was made up of a few villages scattered like seeds around the Acropolis. This flat-topped marble mountain which eventually served as a fortress, now stood before Paul. From a distance it looked like a heavy weight pinning down papyrus sheets on a desk.

In time the citizens of those first few villages conquered their neighbors. But instead of selling their prisoners of war into slavery as was the custom, these progressive Athenians made them into full citizens. Following the success of this radical experiment, a tiny seed of democracy began to grow.

Now, as Paul approached and viewed the Acropolis, his eyes paused for a long moment on the celebrated Parthenon, which dominated the top of the mountain like a magnificently carved, oblong box. Paul had seen many of the fine buildings erected by Herod the Great, but this was equal if not better than any of them.

The marble building with its eight columns in front and back and with six on each side had been erected in honor of Athene during the golden age of Pericles who had ruled the city for thirty-one years.

The actual building was started by the order of Pericles in 447 B.C. It was an age of building temples and each

Athens

Greek city tried to outdo the other—even though the expense nearly bankrupted them.

Pericles had had a problem with the Parthenon. This had to do with its location. The priests insisted that it be built over the ruins of the old temple of Athene which the Persians had destroyed. But Pericles was obstinate. He insisted on the site used by Themistocles for his unfinished Hectompedon, so named because he had planned to make it one hundred feet long.

The next obstacle was money. When it came time to vote on whether or not to allocate funds for this project, it seemed certain that Pericles' plans would be defeated by the Assembly. But at the most dramatic moment, according to Plutarch, Pericles stunned them. "Very, well," he said, "let the cost of these buildings go not to your account but to mine; *and let the inscription on them stand in my name.*"

This suggestion shook the wise ones to the very tips of their beards and turned the tide in favor of Pericles. And so the money—seven hundred talents, perhaps $10,000,000 in our inflated currency—was promptly voted!

Marble for the temple was chosen from that which was quarried at Mt. Pentelicus. No mortar was used anywhere, and since the marble chosen had a fine, iron grain, it was very attractive. Each of the outside columns was six feet, two inches at the base, and nearly thirty-five feet tall. Since the joints in these columns are so perfectly matched, tourists have wondered how it was done. The answer is simple. Each "drum" that formed a section of the column was precisely cut and polished. Then a small hole was drilled into the exact center. Next, a round section of olive-wood was driven into this hole. A second drum was then fitted onto this one and rotated until its surface ground into the section beneath. With patience, the joints became almost invisible.

But the precise joints are not the great marvel wrapped in this work. Aiming at mathematical and artistic beauty, the planners arranged for the columns to be slightly larger

Athens

halfway up, and then to gradually taper toward the top. This was done in order to adjust the straight lines of the temple to the "round eye of man." Likewise, all straight lines were bent just a tiny bit.

These facts indicate that the sculptors and architects of the time had an uncanny understanding of optics and mathematics.

The main purpose of the Parthenon, however, was not just to be a beautiful building. Rather, its main purpose was to house the thirty-eight foot high statue of Athena made of ivory and gold.

Other buildings also stood on the Acropolis, and one wonders what went through Paul's mind as he viewed them. Is it possible that he remembered how Peter had said to the Sanhedrin, "This is the stone which was set at nought of you builders, which is become the head of the corner" (Acts 4:11)? Perhaps!

Having a large Jewish population, Athens had a number of synagogues, and Paul, as usual, took advantage of this fact. Entering one of these public buildings, he preached Jesus Christ to the usually tolerant Greeks. He also preached Christ in the markets. It was in one of these that he came face to face with the Stoics and Eipcureans.

The Stoics were followers of Zeno who had preached in Athens three centuries before. The basic point of his philosophy was to accept all circumstances of life, even poverty and slavery, with a cheerful shrug. And many Athenians accepted this thinking. Indeed, it was even adopted by the Roman Emperor Marcus Aurelius.

The Epicureans had many of the same beliefs as the Stoics. But they liked to emphasize that happiness comes from mental quiet and the absence of fear of the gods. They denied the resurrection vehemently.

Both groups listened to Paul and promptly dubbed him a babbler "because he preached unto them Jesus, and the resurrection" (Acts 17:18).

But with the toleration of Socrates within their beings,

Athens

Like Paul, the modern visitor approaches the Areopagus, where the supreme tribunal of Athens met, to stand on Mars' Hill and look over at the fifth century B.C. Parthenon on the Acropolis, which housed the many statues of the Greek gods and goddesses.

Athens

they were willing to give Paul a chance, and so they "brought him unto the Areopagus" for a hearing.

Since the Areopagus—Mars' Hill—was near the Parthenon, Paul was obliged to climb the Acropolis. And in his day there was a constant stream of Athenians who climbed the hill to present their prayers and offerings to the gods—especially to Athena in the Parthenon. The way to the top was lined with statues of many of the gods, for the Athenians were quite thorough and did not want to neglect the worship of any of them. A vengeful god could cause trouble!

Soon Paul took his place on a flat, marble boulder. With the Parthenon and other marble buildings that had been built to honor the gods on one side, and the sprawling city below, he was ready.

"Ye men of Athens," he began, "I perceive that in all things ye are too superstitious. For as I passed by, and beheld your devotions, I found an altar with this inscription, TO THE UNKNOWN GOD. Whom therefore ye ignorantly worship, him declare I unto you" (Acts 17:22, 23).

With this as a springboard, he preached Christ. But although he knew that he was on "trial" before some of the finest minds of the city, he did not soften his message. Surrounded by idols though he was, and with the marble homes of idols nearby, he was extremely candid: "Forasmuch then as we are the offspring of God, we ought not to think that the Godhead is like unto gold, or silver, or stone, graven by art and man's device" (Acts 17:29).

He then told them about coming judgment and the resurrection of Jesus Christ.

The mention of the resurrection so irritated some in the crowd they began to mock him. But others, interested in this "new" doctrine, said, "We will hear thee again of this matter" (Acts 17:32).

Altars to THE UNKNOWN GOD were in many ancient cities. H. V. Morton relates a curious story in his work, *In the Steps of St. Paul*. "Everyone knew the story of the

Athens

plague that visited Athens in the sixth century before Christ; and how, after sacrifices had been made to every known god and the plague continued, the services of . . . Epimenides, were requested. He drove a flock of black and white sheep to the Areopagus and allowed them to stray from there as they liked, waiting until they rested of their own free will: and on these spots were the sheep sacrificed 'to the fitting god.' The plague ceased, and it became the custom, not in Athens alone, to erect altars to unknown deities."

It has been frequently claimed that Paul's sermon in Athens was a failure. But this is not really true, for several people were converted during the hearing, and a new church was planted in a thriving city. However, Paul felt he should leave and so he continued on to Corinth.

In comparison to the rugged features of Paul, the polished marble houses on the Acropolis seemed mighty indeed. But as the years eddied by, the Athenians learned that the truth preached by this man of Tarsus was sharper than the chisels of the sculptors—and more enduring.

Sometime during the fifth century the statue of Athena disappeared from the Parthenon, and no one knows what happened to it. Also, about this time, the seeming impossible took place. The Parthenon was converted by the Athenians into a Christian church! And it remained a church for approximately one thousand years.

Then in 1456 Athens was conquered by the Turks and converted into a Moslem city. At the beginning of their rule, the Moslems attached a minaret to the Parthenon and used it as a mosque. Later, the Turks used this former home of Athena to store gunpowder.

Next, in 1687 the Venetians found themselves at war with the Turks, and during a battle they attacked the Acropolis. Amidst the shooting a cannon ball went into the Parthenon and touched off the powder. The explosion shattered the roof, blew out some of the walls and caused general havoc.

Thus the building which had endured twenty-one

Athens

centuries, and had survived the attacks of the Romans and barbarians, fell to the aim of a single cannoneer. But this wasn't the worst disaster that was to befall this priceless work of art.

With the shattered remains of the Parthenon lying about like so many crushed eggs, the people were ruthless with the treasures on the ground at their feet. The Turks ground many of the marble gods into gravel for their roads, and many a statue was used by a peasant for a post in his goat pen!

Fortunately for lovers of art, Lord Elgin received permission from the Turkish Government in 1816 to gather the fragments of the Acropolis and ship them to the British Museum.

Thus, many of the statues seen by Paul may now be viewed by anyone who cares to enter the room where they are displayed. There are other rooms in the same museum, however, where one may view ancient Bibles. Strangely enough, the words Paul preached to the Athenians are well preserved in those Bibles while the marbled gods whom the Athenians were worshiping at the time, have either perished in the form of gravel, or are lingering as fragments in a museum. Moreover, many of the people who read Paul's words in the manuscripts believe them, but practically no one today believes in the Greek gods.

In addition to this, those who visit Mars' Hill are now confronted with the message of Paul which he delivered there. That message has been firmly engraved in metal for all to see.

CHAPTER 4

Corinth

When Paul visited Corinth in A.D. 50 or 51, he had no way of knowing that God was about to use him to bring about within this modern city the birth of a great and influential congregation. Nor did he know that this city was to witness the birth of Christian literature. From a human point of view, these things seemed utterly impossible.

Indeed, if the great apostle had been dominated by recent experience, he would have crumpled with discouragement, for his mission to Athens, as we have seen, was not an immediate, glittering success. And here in Corinth he would face the same type of sneering Greeks who had mocked him on Mars' Hill.

Paul, however, trusted in faith—not in experience! And so, the moment he stepped into *Laus Julia Corinthiensis*—the official Roman name—small and then wider doors began to swing wide for him. As a matter of fact, considering everything, Paul's journey to Corinth was one of the most productive journeys of history.

Fortunately for us, the ruins of Corinth remain and one can still see some of the same sights, and feel some of the

Corinth

same pressures that were seen and felt by Paul. Likewise, one can even see the name of one of his converts printed on a paving stone. This printed name is an indication that many influential people were won to Christ at Corinth through his preaching.

The old city of Corinth—the one known by Paul—is just a little over fifty miles directly west of Athens. Today, an excellent highway connects the two cities.

Along this modern highway, just before your arrival in Corinth, you will cross the Corinth Canal. This four-mile-long waterway cuts like a knife across the narrow isthmus that joins the Peloponnesus to Attica. Thus it shortens by two hundred miles the distance ships must travel from the Adriatic ports to Piraeus—the seaport of Athens.

Nero planned this canal in A.D. 66—a few months before the execution of Paul, if one is to believe the current tradition in modern Rome concerning the date of his death. H. V. Morton has described the incident: "On an appointed day the Emperor (Nero) left Corinth at the head of a brilliant gathering and, reaching the site of the canal, snatched up a lyre and sang an ode in honor of Neptune and Amphitrite. He was then handed a golden spade. To the sound of music, he thrust the spade into the earth and collected the sods in a basket which he slung on his back. He then made a speech to the assembled laborers, among whom were six thousand Jews recently captured by Vespasian in the lake-side villages of Galilee, where the Jewish War had begun. It is strange to think that the work of digging in the Corinth Canal was begun by Jewish prisoners of war whose fathers and grandfathers had no doubt heard our Lord preaching on the Sea of Galilee."

Nero, however, abandoned the project. Perhaps he did this because of a superstition that the sea on one side is higher than the sea on the other side. Two years later he committed suicide.

The present canal was started by the French in 1882 and completed by the Greeks eleven years later. In Paul's day, the Romans used an incredible system to cross the

Corinth

isthmus. They moved the ship from one side to the other on rollers!

As far as New Testament evidence is concerned, Paul was alone when he approached the city. Timothy and Silvanus had been sent to Macedonia to check on the churches at Philippi and Thessalonica. The Corinth which Paul entered was a fairly new city. It was just over one hundred years old.

The general area occupied by Corinth, however, had been inhabited as far back as 5000 B.C. Located in a strategic area for trade, blessed with a vast supply of spring water, and surrounded by the fertile Corinthian plain, it was an ideal place in which to live.

Another attraction to settlers was the flat-topped, Lion-colored Acrocorinth mountain which jutted 1875 feet upward just behind the city. This huge mass of rock provided an excellent tower from which to observe an enemy. It was also a convenient place of refuge. And perhaps this is the source of the city's name. Corinth means lookout or guard.

The first sizable number of Greeks moved there about 1000 B.C. From then on, Corinth grew until it was the largest city in Greece. It did not retain this lead, however, for along about the sixth and fifth century B.C. Athens acquired more foreign trade and Corinth became the number two city. Even so, Corinth remained prosperous until 146 B.C. At this time the Roman consul attacked. He captured and utterly destroyed the city. The men were slaughtered, the women and children were sold into slavery.

Following this catastrophe, the razed and dismantled city remained desolate for nearly one hundred years.

But the indomitable career of Corinth had not ended. In 44 B.C. Julius Caesar had it rebuilt as a Roman colony. Next, he colonized it with freedmen and settlers from Italy. Soon the forces that had made the city great in the beginning began to ferment again, and by the time Paul arrived it is estimated that Corinth, together with its

Corinth

The Lechaion Road connected Corinth to the port of Lechaion on the Corinthian Gulf. Once lined with marble columns, it was a magnificent avenue over which endless supplies were carried. The Apostle Paul undoubtedly walked on this road.

Corinth

The Acrocorinth, the flat-topped mountain behind Corinth, is 1875 feet high. It was an extremely strong fortress for the city, and in Paul's day it was topped by a temple to Aphrodite, which was served by one thousand prostitute priestesses.

Corinth

double ports, had a population of nearly 600,000.

The Corinth that Paul witnessed was a new one built on Roman lines. The Lechaion Road, for example, was forty feet wide. It was paved with slabs of hard "slightly colored limestone from the Acrocorinthian quarries." There were sidewalks on either side and smooth gutters to drain away the water from the eaves of the colonnades. And whenever there was a steep rise in the street, broad, easy to ascend steps were installed. This street was for pedestrians only. Thus the marks of wheels that mar the streets of Pompeii are not seen on the Lechaion Road.

The city had a vile reputation for debauchery. At the rear of a colonnade one hundred feet long, there were thirty-three taverns. The city had many night clubs, and standing on the summit of Acrocorinth was the Temple of Aphrodite. This temple employed one thousand priestesses—that is, temple prostitutes.

The reputation of Corinth throughout the Empire was so vile that to insinuate that a man was a "Corinthian" was to insult him. The term applied to gross immorality.

Without a board to forward financial help, Paul had to earn his own living. But this was easy to do in Corinth—the center of the Greek textile industry. Soon he found himself employed on the staff of Aquila and Priscilla. This couple operated a tent-making establishment. Recently expelled from Rome through an edict of Claudius Caesar against the Jews, they were glad to help another stranger in the big city. Also, it may be that they had become Christians while in Rome.

Soon Paul was preaching in the synagogue. Then Timothy and Silvanus appeared with glowing reports from Macedonia. The recently established churches were doing well. Excited with this good news, Paul preached with an even greater intensity and "testified... that Jesus was Christ" (Acts 18:5).

But again the Jews would not tolerate such a statement. And so the synagogue was barred to Paul. However, another door opened almost immediately, and this was the

Corinth

home of Titus Justus, a Roman convert to Judaism "whose house joined hard to the synagogue" (Acts 18:7).

Success followed at once. "And Crispus, the chief ruler of the synagogue, believed on the Lord Jesus with all his house; and many of the Corinthians hearing believed, and were baptized" (Acts 18:8).

These victories in Corinth, however, could not keep Paul's mind from drifting back to Macedonia. Those infant churches were close to his heart. Finally, unable to bear the separation any longer, he dipped his pen and wrote: "Paul, and Silvanus, and Timotheus, unto the church of the Thessalonians" (I Thessalonians 1:1).

Paul, at the time, may not have realized it, but those words were the very first words to be written which would be included in our New Testament. The date of this letter can be set at approximately A.D. 50—and we can be quite dogmatic about the date. Why? Because in Acts 18 we read: "And when Gallio was deputy of Achaia [Corinth was the capitol], the Jews made insurrection with one accord against Paul, and brought him to the judgment seat... And when Paul was now about to open his mouth, Gallio said unto the Jews, If it were a matter of wrong or wicked lewdness, O ye Jews, reason would that I should bear with you: But if it be a question of words and names, and of your law, look ye to it: for I will be no judge of such matters" (verses 12-15).

The problem now is to pin down the date when Gallio was deputy of Achaia. And fortunately this is possible through an inscription found at Delphi. That inscription narrows Gallio's tenure to this period. Alas, Gallio along with his two brothers, Mela and Seneca, was put to death about A.D. 66 through the orders of Nero. This was in spite of the fact that Seneca had been Nero's tutor. (Gallio was forced to commit suicide, and this he did by opening his veins and then lying in a tub of warm water. This was the popular method of the time.)

First and Second Thessalonians, however, were not the only letters that Paul wrote while he was in Corinth. While

Corinth

on his third missionary journey, Paul returned to Corinth and wrote his longest and most influential work—the book of Romans.

Curiously, when Paul wrote to the Corinthians, he exclaimed, "I thank God that I baptized none of you, but Crispus and Gaius" (I Corinthians 1:14). And then in concluding the book of Romans, he mentions that Gaius was his host. Thus, there is strong evidence that Paul wrote—or rather dictated—the manuscript while boarding with one of the two whom he had baptized.

Romans has some strong passages against immorality, and one can easily imagine that Paul composed them after a morning stroll in which his eyes rested on the Temple of Aphrodite on the summit of Acrocorinth.

In the final chapter of Romans where Paul gives credit to Gaius—16:23—he also said, "Erastus the chamberlain of the city saluteth you . . ."

Today, one of the paving blocks in the ruins of Corinth has written on it the following inscription:

ERASTVS PRO AEDILITATE
S P STRAVIT

Interpreted from Latin, this reads: "Erastus, in return for his aedilship, laid the pavement at his own expense." (Aedilship is Latin for commissioner of the streets and public buildings.)

Was this the Erastus to whom Paul referred? Many researchers think so. At least archaeologists think that the inscription was in existence during the first century after Christ.

Today there is a new Corinth. It is a little to the east of the old one. But for one reason or another, it is just a modest town of 10,000.

CHAPTER 5

Philippi

As the inter-island ship rocked along through the blue Aegean Sea, Paul and his companions must have tingled with excitement, for after a series of closed doors the Holy Spirit had definitely directed them to Europe. And as a scholar, Paul knew that Europe needed the gospel. No one could deny that.

The preceding days of uncertainty in Asia were now over, and before them lay the Macedonian port of Neapolis—and then, ten miles inland, the ancient city of Philippi. Named in honor of Philip II of Macedon, the one-eyed father of Alexander the Great, it was a spine-tingling place, for in its streets and swamps world history had been battered and twisted into many a new shape. A city of giants and blood, it was almost equivalent to Gettysburg, Verdun, and Waterloo all rolled into one.

In 334 B.C., using Philippi as one of his European bases, Alexander the Great had invaded Asia. Now, in stark contrast, Paul, using Asia as his base, planned to invade Europe with the sword of the Spirit. Moreover, this God-intoxicated man from Tarsus was certain of success.

As the ship continued westward toward the flaming sun

Philippi

behind Mount Athos, Paul's assurance increased. The three who traveled with him were of the highest type. Silas, whom he insisted on calling Silvanus, had the confidence of the brethren in both Jerusalem and Antioch, and Timothy who had joined the band at Lystra was so useful Paul called him "his beloved son." The fourth member was Luke, who had united with Paul at Troas under the most unique circumstances.

On this, his second missionary journey, Paul had planned to visit such cities as Ephesus, Philadelphia, Sardis, and Miletus. But as he wearied along "they ... were forbidden of the Holy Ghost to preach the word in Asia" (Acts 16:6). Paul, however, was reluctant to give up and so he decided to go to Bithynia. That long province, warmed by the *Pontus Euxinus*—Black Sea—was a rich and fruitful area. (If the borders of this Roman province were still intact, they would include the Asiatic part of Istanbul.) But again he was prevented. This time, "the Spirit suffered them not. And they passing by Mysia came down to Troas" (Acts 16:7,8).

Why the *Holy Spirit* stopped them at one place and the *Spirit of Jesus* in another place is a mystery for the scholars. Undoubtedly both references are to the Holy Spirit. But perhaps on the second occasion the feeling of being forbidden was so strong, Paul was reminded of his experience on the Damascus Road when the voice of Jesus said, "Saul, Saul, why persecutest thou me?" (Acts 9:4). That appeal brought about the most radical change in his life. It turned him from a persecutor into a proclaimer. Likewise, the closed door to Bithynia and the call to Europe entailed a radical change.

It was in Troas that the Holy Spirit's directions came to him in the most dramatic form. "And a vision appeared to Paul in the night; There stood a man of Macedonia, and prayed him, saying, Come over into Macedonia, and help us (Acts 16:9). Moderns remember Troas as the place where Paul received the startling invitation to Macedonia. But in earlier centuries, Troas was associated with nearby Troy made famous by Homer's story about Helen and the

Philippi

Trojan's wooden horse.

Following the vision, Luke suddenly appeared, and in his account of the voyage as recorded in Acts, he began to use the pronoun "we" at this place. This means that he was now traveling with Paul, and that what we read is an eyewitness account. A doctor, a scholar, and a great writer, was Luke, and Paul had so much confidence in him he referred to him as "the beloved physician."

Remembering the trip, Luke wrote: "Therefore loosing from Troas, we came with a straight course to Samothracia, and the next day to Neapolis; And from thence to Philippi, which is the chief city of that part of Macedonia, and a colony" (Acts 16:11,12).

The sails of the ship must have been taut in order to make the trip in two days, for on a reverse voyage—sailing from Philippi to Troas—it took five days! (Acts 20:6).

Enjoying a straight run to Samothrace is interesting, for all ships making this crossing have to face a strong southward current from Cape Helles. Today, the island of Samothrace, where they stopped in mid-voyage, is remembered as the place where the exquisite statue, Winged Victory, was discovered in 1863. It may be that Paul and his friends even saw it, for it had been mounted for public view by Demetrius in 305 B.C.

Always a student, Paul's blood must have churned as he walked down the colonnaded streets of Philippi, viewed the great amphitheater, paused in front of the marble-columned buildings, felt the cool spray of the fountains, and chatted with the proud inhabitants.

Prior to 361 B.C., the city was known as Krenides. Then in 356 B.C. King Philip II of Macedonia sent in a sizable number of colonists. The gold mines in the vicinity were part of the lure. Philip gave the town his own name and made it an outpost against the Thracians.

Nearly two centuries later in 168 B.C. Macedonia was conquered by the Romans and divided into four sections with Philippi as part of the first. And then Brutus and Cassius—assassins of Julius Caesar—clashed with the armies of Octavian and Antony just west of the city.

Philippi

Strolling through Philippi was like viewing a museum dedicated to history! Indeed, one can imagine an oldster tottering up to Paul and saying, "Come! Let me show you where the armies stood. My grandfather fought here. Over there is where—"

The story of this battle where the Roman Republic perished was painfully clear to Paul, for he was from Tarsus. And the citizens of Tarsus had every reason to remember.

Following Caesar's assassination, Cassius—the main instigator of the plot—and his brother-in-law Brutus fled from Rome. Without considering the consequences, the Roman Senate had given them the province of Macedonia and Cyrene. And now the two assassins began to raise armies so that they could defeat Octavian and Antony and become the sole rulers of the Empire.

Armies, however, cost money; and since neither Brutus nor Cassius had any, they devised a system to raise it in a hurry. They forced the cities they controlled to pay their taxes ten years in advance! In addition, they murdered the wealthy and seized their estates. Cassius moved to Tarsus, quartered his soldiers in the homes, and coldly announced that he wouldn't leave until he was paid $9,000,000.

To raise this amount—in those days a fantastic sum—public lands were auctioned, silver and gold vessels from the temples were melted, and the free were sold into slavery. First to be enslaved were boys, then girls, then men and women, and finally old people. Many killed themselves rather than submit. Born between A.D. 10 and 15, Paul must have heard many a spine-tingling tale from those who had been affected by such outrage.

Judea, too, felt this injustice. There, Cassius demanded $4,200,000 and sold the entire population of four towns into slavery.

Brutus, likewise, was ruthless. "When the citizens of Lycian Xanthus refused his demands, he besieged them until, starving but obdurate, they committed suicide en masse" (Will Durant in *Caesar and Christ*).

In September of 42 B.C. the rival armies flooded into

Philippi

Philippi. The camp of Brutus—forming the right wing—was on high ground in front of the city and extended to the mountain across the Egnatian Way. Followers of Cassius manned the left wing—also on high ground. Their fortifications extended into the damp marshes and across that part of the Egnatian Way that connects Philippi to the Symbolon ridge. Cassius also had a lookout on a hill just northeast of Philippi.

Antony and his army reached Philippi by following the Egnatian Way from the west. They camped on the lower, marshy ground in front of Cassius and Brutus. Octavian, who had been ill, arrived in a litter. Together, he and Antony had nineteen legions plus auxiliaries.

Militarily, Octavian and Antony were at a disadvantage. Not only were Brutus and Cassius on higher ground, but they could also get supplies from Asia by way of the sea. In contrast, their rivals could only get supplies from Macedonia—and there was not much available.

With their spears and shields glistening in the sun, the armies glowered at each other for an entire month without making a move. Ghosts bothered Brutus. And Cassius was wary because of the vultures which circled the camp. Cassius knew that Octavian was short of supplies, and because of this, he felt it best to wait and starve him out.

But Brutus was nervous and begged to attack. Cassius pointed to a swarm of bees on one of his standards. This, he declared, was a terrible omen. Brutus, nevertheless, was determined and so the battle started. The army of Brutus, like a race horse, was too anxious. The men charged before the signal. Then a group slipped around Octavian's flank, killed the guards, and jabbed their spears through his litter again and again until they felt assured that he was dead.

In spite of this strong beginning, however, Cassius and Brutus were defeated, and Octavian, warned through the dream of a friend, had been away when his litter was attacked. Cornered, Cassius commanded his freedman to kill him. Brutus also committed suicide.

Philippi

At dawn, when Antony viewed the corpse of Brutus, he unbuckled his scarlet general's coat and spread it over the body. Years before, he and Brutus had been friends. But Octavian was not so thoughtful. He hacked off his enemy's head and sent it to Rome to be placed at the foot of Julius Caesar's statue.

Eleven years later, Octavian and Antony—Cleopatra's new lover—went to war against each other. And then during the battle of Actium, off the west coast of Greece, Octavian utterly defeated the fleets of Antony and Cleopatra. Next, Antony and Cleopatra committed suicide. This left Octavian the undisputed emperor of Rome. Four years later the Senate voted him the title of Augustus, and he remained on the throne from 31 B.C. to 14 A.D.

While seeking God's will in Philippi, Paul must have pondered long over these events. But with his knowledge of Jesus, he refused to be bound by a past that had reddened the streets of the city. His eyes were on the future.

Early questioning had shown that there was no synagogue in the city. This was an indication that the Jewish population was extremely small, for generally when there was a minimum of ten male Jews there was also a synagogue. But Paul soon discovered that there was a place of prayer by the riverside where a number of women gathered to worship each Sabbath.

Unlike the rival generals in the Battle of Philippi who simply stared at each other for an entire month, Paul was not afraid to make the first move. And so when the Sabbath came, the team headed for the river just outside the city gate of Philippi. One can imagine Paul's mounting excitement as he strode forward on his way to teach the first Christian lesson that had ever been taught by an apostle on the European continent.

That he would be speaking to a crowd of ladies which included at least one rich one must have been a disturbing thought, for his memory of a previous situation was not pleasant. While in Antioch of Pisidia he was enjoying unusual success when some "women of standing" nearly

Philippi

The river Angites flows just west of the present ruins of Philippi. It was in this river that Lydia was baptized. Nearby, the modern visitor can stay in the Hotel Lydia, even as Paul and his companions were constrained to abide in Lydia's home.

Philippi

ruined everything. Indeed, they drove him from the city.

The possibility that these women would turn on him was great. And if they did so, they could ruin his ministry in Macedonia.

As Paul faced the women on the shallow river—probably the Angites—he did so as a veteran of Christ. Soon there was a silence as the women began to listen to this intense man of Tarsus and his friends. (Remember Luke recorded "we went out of the city by a river side, where prayer was wont to be made; and we sat down, and spake unto the women which resorted thither," Acts 16:13).

Among the listeners was "Lydia, a seller of purple, of the city of Thyatira, which worshipped God" (Acts 16:14). The fact that Lydia was a dealer in purple indicates that she was a person of means, for purple was one of the most coveted commodities of the time. The name Canaan (Land of the Purple) was derived from this dye, and Phoenicia comes from a Greek word meaning red-purple. Sir William Ramsay estimated that a pound of wool dyed in purple was worth forty English pounds.

The dye was made from the secretions of the hypobranchial glands of certain mollusks, and the different shades were achieved by using various species of the same family of shellfish.

Obtaining the dye was extremely difficult process, but since the demand was great—it was used in the Tabernacle and in the Temple and by the rich—no trouble was spared to obtain it.

The nationality of Lydia is unknown. Perhaps she was a convert to Judaism. All we know is that she was a worshiper of God. But as she listened to Paul, she was convinced that he was telling the truth and her "heart the Lord opened, that she attended unto the things which were spoken of Paul" And thus she became the first known person to be converted on European soil.

Having experienced the new birth, Lydia became an enthusiastic believer, and soon she and her entire household were baptized. Bubbling with joy, she confronted the

Philippi

team. "If ye have judged me to be faithful to the Lord," she said, "come into my house, and abide there" (Acts 16:15). And Luke added with his marvelous touch, "and she constrained us."

The first church to be planted in Europe was having a marvelous start. Then trouble swooped down from an unexpected source. While the team was on its way to pray, a demon-possessed girl suddenly appeared in the streets. The girl was being led around by her owners. Such sights in a land that believed in oracles was common.

A typical girl like this would speak in a high-pitched voice to a customer, and then her masters would interpret the message for a small fee. With thousands anxious to know the future, it was a profitable business.

Pointing to the missionaries, the girl began to shout, "These men are the servants of the most high God, which shew unto us the way of salvation" (Acts 16:17).

At first Paul and his friends ignored it, but the girl continued to follow and repeat her announcement. Finally, his patience exhausted, Paul said to the spirit that was troubling her, "I command thee in the name of Jesus Christ to come out of her." And Luke adds, "and he came out the same hour" (Acts 16:18).

Incensed because the girl now refused to tell fortunes, the owners seized Paul and Silas "and drew them into the marketplace unto the rulers." Great writer that he was, Luke does not waste words. In this incident, he points out by omitting the names of the others, that only Paul and Silas were arrested. And this makes us wonder why they didn't seize Timothy and Luke. A suggestion is that Paul and Silas resembled Jews more than the others, and since they were being persecuted by Gentiles, this may be the correct explanation. Timothy had a Greek father and Luke was a Gentile.

Undoubtedly the city was anti-Semitic. After the Battle of Philippi, Octavian had settled the area with veterans of the war and had given the inhabitants unique Roman citizenship privileges. Also, he had changed the name of the city to a flattering new one—*Colonia August Julia*

Philippi

Philippensis! At the time of Paul's visit—sometime between A.D. 49 and 52—Emperor Claudius was on the throne, and he had expelled the Jews from Rome. Since Philippi boasted on being "Little Rome," its leaders were quick to follow the laws of the bigger city.

At the public square, the accusers did not waste time. In caustic racist language they said: "These men, being Jews, do exceedingly trouble our city, And teach customs, which are not lawful for us to receive, neither to observe, being Romans" (Acts 16:20,21). Luke then describes what happened. "And the multitude rose up together against them: and the magistrates rent off their clothes, and commanded to beat them. And when they had laid many stripes upon them, they cast them into prison, charging the jailor to keep them safely; Who, having received such a charge, thrust them into the inner prison, and made their feet fast in the stocks" (Acts 16:22-24).

The worst American prisons are palaces in comparison to some of the prisons in the old Roman Empire. With poor ventilation, scanty sanitary facilities, and the worst kind of food, a prisoners' life was a tortured existence. But Paul and Silas were in an even more miserable situation than usual, for in addition to the pain from their wounds their legs were clamped in the stocks, making sleep impossible. Definitely, it was time to complain. But instead of grieving, they sang!

There were other prisoners in the jail, and one can imagine how they may have grumbled at the joyful sounds of the two preachers. But nothing could silence Paul and Silas. The church had been planted in Europe, and they were being strengthened by the risen Christ! Then "at midnight" there "was a great earthquake, so that the foundations of the prison were shaken: and immediately all the doors were opened, and every one's bands were loosed" (Acts 16:26).

On the human level this seems an incredible story, for how could an earthquake remove stocks from the prisoners' feet? Sir William Ramsay, however, has an adequate explanation. "Anyone that has seen a Turkish

Philippi

prison will not wonder that the doors were thrown open: each door was merely closed by a bar, and the earthquake, as it passed along the ground, forced the door posts apart from each other, so that the bar slipped from its hold, and the door swung open. The prisoners were fastened to the wall or in wooden stocks; and the chains and stocks were detached from the wall, which was so shaken that space gaped between the stones" *(St. Paul the Traveler and the Roman Citizen).*

Immediately they were freed, and Paul and Silas might have fled. At the time of Peter's arrest by the order of Herod, this is exactly what he did. But if Paul and Silas had fled, they probably would not have gotten away, for unlike Peter they were in a Gentile city where their Jewish features made them obvious. Moreover, they were being guided by the Holy Spirit. It was in God's plan for Peter to escape, but it was not in God's plan for Paul to escape!

Awakening from his sleep, the jailer was shocked to see the prison doors flung wide. Assuming his prisoners had escaped, he started to commit suicide. But noticing his action, Paul shouted, "Do thyself no harm: for we are all here." The startled jailer then called for lights, "sprang in, and came trembling, and fell down before Paul and Silas" (Acts 16:28,29).

At this point, critics wonder how Paul could see the jailer without a light, and yet the jailer had to have a light to see Paul. The answer is simple. Paul and Silas had been sitting in the darkness. In addition, it is easier to notice violent movement in the semidarkness of starlight than to see the features of a man's face.

The jailer, perhaps a son or grandson of a veteran of the Battle of Philippi, may have had the typical Roman fears of omens. Also, his conscience may have been disturbed for placing these noted prisoners in the stocks. But regardless of the source of his fears, he cried out and said, 'Sirs, what must I do to be saved?'"

Prepared by song and prayer, Paul and Silas had an immediate answer, "Believe on the Lord Jesus Christ, and thou shalt be saved, and thy house." And then, following

Philippi

their advice, Paul and Silas "spake unto him the word of the Lord, and to all that were in his house" (Acts 16:31,32).

Deeply repenting of his sins, the jailer washed their wounds, "and was baptized, he and all his, straightway" (verse 33). Were they baptized in the same place where Lydia was baptized? It is entirely possible, for the river was within walking distance. Luke, however, does not mention the place. But he does tell us that the jailer "brought them into his house, he set meat before them, and rejoiced, believing in God with all his house" (verse 34). As a doctor, Luke was interested in their health!

At daylight the magistrates sent officers with instructions to release the prisoners. But Paul refused to be released! "They have beaten us openly uncondemned, being Romans, and have cast us into prison; and now do they thrust us out privily? nay verily; but let them come themselves and fetch us out" (verse 37).

No, Paul was not trying to be difficult. But he was anxious for the new congregation to have a good name in the city!

Thoroughly frightened, the magistrates came and apologized and begged them to leave the city. Now that they were legally free, the former prisoners returned to Lydia's house, "and when they had seen the brethren, they comforted them, and departed" (verse 40).

And thus, amidst misunderstanding and suffering, Europe's first church was founded. Luke's "we" passages end abruptly at this point, and do not continue again until Acts 20:6 where we read, "And we sailed away from Philippi after the days of unleavened bread, and came unto them to Troas in five days; where we abode seven days."

The obvious conclusion is that Luke was left in Philippi to strengthen the church. This conclusion is firmed by II Corinthians 8:18, where Paul said: "And we have sent with him the brother, whose praise is in the gospel throughout all the churches." According to early tradition, this passage referred to Luke.

CHAPTER 6

Thessalonica

Urgently requested by the magistrates to leave Philippi at once, Paul and Silas, and perhaps Timothy, headed southwest on the Egnatian Way for Thessalonica. Having been severely beaten in Philippi, Paul and Silas must have been in pain as they trudged along.

The first large city on the way was Amphipolis—about twenty miles from Philippi. Today, this city rates less than one hundred words in a typical Bible dictionary. This is because there is no New Testament record of a church being founded there. However, the city did have a Christian witness in the succeeding years. This we know because remains of a Christian community were unearthed in 1920. Today, the city has disappeared.

But during Paul's time, Amphipolis—on the left bank of the Strymon—enjoyed a certain fame, especially with history buffs. The family of the Greek historian Thucydides—460 to 400 B.C.—owned mining rights there; and following the Roman conquest, it eventually was made the capital of that part of Macedonia.

In addition, Amphipolis had supplied Alexander the Great with three of his star naval officers: Nearchos,

Thessalonica

The modern visitor has the interesting experience of staying comfortably in new Thessalonica (known today as Salonica) while searching out the history of the ancient city which Paul knew.

Thessalonica

Androsthenes, and Laomedon. In 1912 a great stone lion was uncovered here, and it is thought that it was erected in honor of Laomedon.

The Ptolemies of Egypt also originated in this city. Another bit of history that was constantly dripping from the loose tongues of the guides concerned the civil war between Pompey—the one who made Palestine a Roman province in 63 B.C.—and his father-in-law, Julius Caesar. Following utter defeat at Pharsalus, Pompey boarded a ship at Amphipolis and sailed for Egypt. In Egypt the defeated general was knifed to death as he stepped ashore.

At the end of another day's journey, Paul and his friends reached Apollonia, an additional thirty miles away. From here it was only thirty-eight miles to Thessalonica. How they traveled, no one knows. It can be assumed they walked.

Thessalonica was the type of city Paul liked to cultivate for Christ. It was the largest commercial center in the southeastern section of Europe. Firmly situated on both the Via Egnatia and the Aegean Sea, it was in easy contact with the rest of the world. Paul believed that a strong congregation here could be a spiritual watershed to other areas.

In the beginning, among the tiny villages at this place, was one named Therma. It was probably so named because of the nearby Thermaic Gulf. Then about 315 B.C., Cassander, a general who had served under Alexander the Great, united the villages into a city. He named the new combination in honor of his wife Thessalonica, a stepsister of Alexander the Great.

Around 168 B.C. Thessalonica, at this time a walled fortress, fell to the Romans in the battle of Pydna. This concluded the Roman conquest of Macedonia. Eighteen years later, Thessalonica was made into the capital of the second of the four districts into which the Romans had divided the country. Next, during the war between Caesar and Pompey about a century later, Pompey used Thessalonica as his base. This means that Thessalonica was deeply associated with the loser, and in those days of

Thessalonica

vengeance this could mean trouble. But the city redeemed itself a short time later when it backed Octavian and Antony in their war against Brutus and Cassius. As a reward for its help, Octavian made Thessalonica a free city.

At the time of Paul's visit, Thessalonica was a prosperous city with a large Jewish colony. Today, Salonica—the modern name—is proud of Paul's visit, and eager guides are anxious to show tourists the place where he entered the city—and the place where he left. According to a legend, when Paul stepped through the gates he knelt to pray. This *very* spot has been marked by a circular piece of marble.

Luke's record of Paul's visit to Thessalonica recorded in Acts has been the basis for serious debate. The first of the problems has to do with Acts 17:6 and 8. In the original, the officials mentioned in these passages were referred to as *politarchs*. This fact was used by critics to support their claim that the book of Acts was unreliable. Part of their claim was because this word is not found elsewhere, or so they thought. Since then, however, at least sixteen examples of the term have been discovered. Indeed, the word was found on a Roman arch in Thessalonica.

Since Thessalonica had been made a free city, the politarchs had the freedom to make their own decisions about internal affairs.

Another problem concerning Paul's visit to Thessalonica has to do with the length of his stay. Since there was a large Jewish population, the city had a synagogue—Paul's favorite place to start a new work. Luke wrote: "And Paul, as his manner was, went in unto them, and three sabbath days reasoned with them out of the scriptures" (Acts 17:2).

Three sabbaths in a row could mean just a little over two weeks—the length of a revival campaign. And yet we have the following facts: (1) A strong church which followed through with a vigorous missionary program was established (I Thessalonians 1:8). (2) Paul got a full-time job at his tent-making trade (I Thessalonians 2:9). (3)

Thessalonica

While in Thessalonica, Paul received two gifts from the church at Philippi (Philippians 4:16).

That all of these accomplishments and activities could be crammed into such a short period seems amazing. And yet all things are possible with the Lord, especially when we are fully surrendered! Moreover, the world-shattering convulsions of Pentecost took place in even less time.

Sir William Ramsay thought that the "three sabbaths" merely referred to the times that Paul taught in the synagogue. Indeed, he was so certain that Paul was in Thessalonica for a longer period, he suggested that he was probably there from December of A.D. 50 to May of 51. And Sir William may be right.

As usual, however, a riot was stirred up. "But the Jews which believed not," wrote Luke, "moved with envy, took unto them certain lewd fellows of the baser sort, and gathered a company, and set all the city on an uproar, and assaulted the house of Jason, and sought to bring them out to the people.

"And when they found them not, they drew Jason and certain brethren unto the rulers of the city, crying, These that have turned the world upside down are coming hither also" (Acts 17:5, 6).

Since Thessalonica was a large city, the fact that it was all in an "uproar" indicates that Paul had made a great impression. And this fact comes to sharp focus when we recognize that the Romans were expert in keeping civil disorders to a minimum.

In the presence of the politarchs, the mob shouted, "These all do contrary to the decrees of Caesar, saying that there is another king, one Jesus" (Acts 17:7).

Insinuating that the Christians had flouted the Emperor, they touched a sensitive spot. True, Thessalonica was a free city. But the accusation of treason carried terrifying implications. Having had a series of semi-sane emperors on the throne, the politarchs were unusually wary. A single word uttered by the Emperor could result in the loss of their freedom or even mass crucifixions. Tacitus declared that Tiberius took in a good share of the Empire's

Thessalonica

income by making such accusations and then forcing the accused to forfeit either their cash or their lives.

Considering the situation, the politarchs acted with mildness when they released Jason and the others on bond.

That evening the congregation sent Paul and Silas off to Berea—some fifty miles to the west. Paul left with a heavy heart.

Berea was a lovely city in Macedonia. Lying at the foot of Mt. Bermius and on a tributary of the Haliacmon, it was one of those places where most people would like to linger. Once again Paul started to preach Christ in the synagogue. And here he found the Jews more receptive. "These were more noble than those in Thessalonica, in that they received the word with all readiness of mind, and searched the scriptures daily" (Acts 17:11).

But once again a mob appeared. This time the ruffians came from Thessalonica, and they caused so much disturbance that Paul felt it wise to move on.

Having been grossly mistreated by the Jews of Thessalonica, Paul might have forgotten the church he had founded. But he did not. Instead, he wrote them a letter from Corinth, and then followed it with another. These letters are known as First and Second Thessalonians. The first of these letters became the very first writing that was gathered into the collection of books that we now call the New Testament. The letters are concerned with the resurrection, death, judgment, obedience—and especially the second coming of Christ.

Paul longed to see the Thessalonian brethren again. In the first letter, he wrote: "Wherefore we would have come unto you, even I Paul, once again; but Satan hindered us" (I Thessalonians 2:18).

How did Satan hinder him? Sir William Ramsay thinks that he was hindered because of the bonds which were extracted from Jason and the others to guarantee that there would be no more disturbances. If Paul had returned there might have been another mob and those bonds would have been forfeited and Jason put into custody.

CHAPTER 7

Ephesus

The Ephesus that Paul knew was a glittering city of wealth, fame, power, incredible superstition—and flagrant sin. It was also the largest Asian city in the Roman Empire. Ships from every nation crowded its ports.

But whatever its commercial attributes might have been, its greatest hold on fame was attached to its Temple of Artemis—also known as the Temple of Diana. And without doubt when Paul arrived in Ephesus in A.D. 52-55, he saw the temple and the eager crowds milling around it. The massive structure with its rows of marble columns was one of the Seven Wonders of the World, and like the Eiffel Tower was almost impossible to avoid.

After visiting it, an ancient traveler was completely overwhelmed. He wrote: "I have seen the walls and hanging gardens of the old Babylon, the statue of Olympian Jove, the Colossus of Rhodes, the great labor of the lofty pyramids, and the ancient tomb of Mausolus. But when I saw the Temple of Ephesus towering to the clouds, all of these marvels were eclipsed."

This temple, however, along with most of the old city

Ephesus

where Paul had walked and labored, disappeared completely from view for many a century, and its existence was so forgotten, crops were cultivated on the soil that covered it. And then J. Turtle Wood, an Englishman, went to Turkey in 1863 to see if he could locate the Temple of Artemis, and the rest of the city.

Attracted by a weed-covered pond, Wood began to sink shafts. But these deep holes revealed nothing of real value. He, however, was an indomitable man, and to find the lost temple became an obsession. Fearlessly he tried again and again. But always without result. And along with discouragement, he had a continuing battle with malaria, thieves, the Turkish government, and a gnawing lack of funds. He was being financed by the British Museum, but its directors were determined not to waste a penny.

As the natives watched him at work, they saw a bearded man dressed in a tightly-buttoned frock coat and crowned with a stovepipe hat. All sorts of ridicule were flung at him by the local population, and a large section of the more illiterate questioned his motives. Perhaps he was out to free evil spirits. Or perhaps all of this digging would unleash another earthquake!

But neither illness, broken bones, nor ridicule could deter J. T. Wood. Finally, after six years of near-fruitless labor, he dug into the theater which is mentioned in Acts 19. There, he uncovered a number of inscriptions which had been written on thin slabs of marble and fastened to the walls.

Among these were copies of letters from the Roman Emperors Hadrian and Antoninus Pius which had been addressed to the Magistrates, Council, and people of Ephesus. One of the letters from Antoninus reproached the Ephesians because they did not agree with the suggestions of Vedius Antoninus who had a plan to improve the city.

These slabs were of historical interest, but they did not give a clue to the location of other important buildings in the city. If only he could find a map!

Ephesus

Then, on clearing the southern entrance to the theater, Wood discovered a long inscription inscribed on several huge blocks of marble which had been carefully dowelled together. This inscription described about thirty silver and gold images, weighing from 3 to 7 pounds each. These images—probably resembling those made by Demetrius—were described by Wood as of "Artemis with two stags, and a variety of emblematical figures."

Undoubtedly this inscription had been placed in this prominent place in order to satisfy the vanity of a certain Roman citizen, C. Vibius Salutarius. This gentleman who had lived in Ephesus some fifty years after Paul's ministry, had presented the Temple of Artemis with these images. In addition, according to the inscription, he had set up an endowment to provide money to keep the images polished!

Ah, but that isn't all that was mentioned. Having provided for the images and their upkeep, the financier insisted on certain procedures. One of these was that on special days, including the birthday of Diana, the images were to be carried in a procession from the temple to the theater. Moreover, he decreed that the procession was to include "two curators of the temple . . . conquerors in the games . . . a staff bearer and guards." He also described the route that was to be followed with extreme care. And in his instructions he mentioned the Magnesian gate and the Coressian gate.

Wood's heart fluttered as he read the long inscription. Intuitively, he realized that this wealthy Roman wanted as many people as possible to see his gifts, and thus he had arranged for the bearers to follow a long, circuitous route. And now if he could only find and identify those gates! He redoubled his efforts.

By the last day of 1869 he had not only discovered the gates, but he had also located the site of the temple. It was a mere twenty feet beneath the top of the ground on a rather modest elevation. At the time, he had been suffering from a three-week attack of malaria. But even

Ephesus

though he had chills and his bones ached, he continued to excavate until he had located a number of columns and the celebrated carved drums. These drums distinguished the Temple of Artemis from other temples in the Greek world and thus proved he had located the correct temple.

The Temple of Artemis has been carefully reconstructed in model form, and from the excavations and passages in ancient literature, its dimensions are quite definitely known. The building was just under 164 feet wide and a little over 342 feet long. Altogether, there were one hundred outside columns. The columns were 6 feet at the base and slightly over 55 feet high. Pliny tells us that 36 of them were sculptured. The roof was of "white marble tile."

The statue of Diana, prominently displayed in the temple, was that of a multibreasted woman, considered a fertility goddess. Also, "the image which fell down from Jupiter" (Acts 19:35)—probably an aerolite—was housed there.

Since the temple was solidly built, it served as a sort of international bank, and it is said that the first type of traveler's checks were issued from here. During the first century, there was an annual month-long festival in honor of Artemis which drew as many as half a million people from all over the Mediterranean world.

Wood's discoveries in Ephesus have all underlined the accuracy of the New Testament—and especially that of Acts.

The history of Ephesus is pitted with almost incredible mystery and legend. It is claimed that the first city was founded three thousand B.C. and that it acquired its name from a fierce Amazon queen. The Amazons—according to legend were from a race of warrior women who captured and enslaved men. And so determined were they, it is claimed, they burned off their right breasts to enable them to draw back their bowstrings farther and shoot their arrows with better ease. (It has been suggested that the idea of the Amazons came into being because Hittite

Ephesus

soldiers on Egyptian monuments are shown wearing robes reaching to the feet.)

Ephesus was their largest city.

By around one thousand B.C. their city had vanished. And then some Athenians decided that they would build a new one. But first they consulted the Delphic Oracle for instructions. There, the mysterious voice told them that a fish would mark the *general* place and that a boar would lead them to the *precise* location.

Soon, a fish jumped out of a fire where it was being roasted. A live coal attached to it set the bushes on fire, and this fire frightened a boar which led the picnickers to the right spot. But legend as this must be, the Ephesians believed it, and as late as A.D. 400 the statue of an honored boar stood just outside the gates!

Extremely well located, Ephesus was an ideal stopping place between East and West. Many important roads met there as did the sea lanes. And then during the reign of Attalus II—one of the kings of Pergamus—an engineer made a serious mistake. Seeking to make the River Cayster scour better, he narrowed the mouth of the stream on the north side, and built an extensive mole into the sea. But his works had an opposite effect to what he had planned.

The surrounding mountains were saturated with loose, disintegrating stone filled with mica-schist. Normally, this debris was washed away by the sea. Now, the narrowed banks and mole stopped this and the harbor began to silt up until it became unusable. This tended to slow the development of Ephesus. The Romans attempted to remove the silt in A.D. 65, but the task proved so enormous they gave up. In time, Smyrna began to replace Ephesus as a seaport.

Jealous of the prosperous Ephesians, the Lydian Croesus launched an attack in the sixth century B.C. The terrified Ephesians sought protection by tying a series of long ropes from the highest part of the temple to the city three-quarters of a mile away. But Artemis was unable to

Ephesus

help them. Croesus then destroyed the city and moved the population further inland toward the temple. Indeed, he repaired the temple and provided a set of column drums with his name inscribed on them. These may be seen in the British Museum.

Following the labors of Croesus, the city and temple continued to expand. Then in 365 B.C., the year Alexander the Great was born, a lunatic by the name of Herostratus, wishing to commemorate his name, set the temple on fire and destroyed it.

Under the spell of Artemis, the Ephesians immediately hired a famous architect—either Deinocrates or Cheirocrates—and began to rebuild on a grand scale. In the midst of construction, Alexander the Great appeared in 334 B.C. Utterly charmed, the youthful conqueror offered to pay the entire cost of reconstruction and to provide funds for perpetual care. However, he had a condition. That condition was that his name be inscribed on the building!

To this request, the Ephesians came up with the world's most diplomatic refusal. It would be wrong, suggested their spokesmen, for one god to make a dedication to another god! Highly pleased with this retort, Alexander directed that the Ephesian tribute money be retained by the city and used for the temple.

Ephesus mushroomed again in size—and pride. About 190 B.C. the Romans defeated Antiochus the Great. They forced him to turn Ephesus over to them, and they in turn gave the city to Eumenes II, king of Pergamos. Next, in 133 B.C., the Romans took the city back and made it the capital of their Asian province. In A.D. 29, Ephesus was severely damaged by an earthquake. Generously, Tiberius hastened to repair the damage—and claim credit on his coins for having done so.

Again and again the temple was damaged. Nevertheless, it was always restored or rebuilt—and generally on a grander scale. Across the centuries, the temple became an asylum where the pursued could find refuge.

Ephesus

For a while, the safety zone was confined to the temple itself. And then Alexander the Great increased the area of refuge by decreeing that anyone who was within a *stade* of the temple was safe. The distance of a stade was determined by Mithridates who shot an arrow from a corner of the roof. This distance of two hundred yards was officially felt to be too long; but being generous, and having a firm faith in Artemis, the rulers did not object.

After Mark Antony occupied Ephesus in 41 B.C. and was joined by Cleopatra, he doubled the radius of the safety zone. This meant that any fugitive who managed to get within four hundred yards of the temple was safe.

The Temple of Artemis, however, did not stop the Ephesians from emperor worship, for Artemis was considered to be merely a god among many gods. As the Roman rule flowered, the emperors insisted that a temple be built for emperor worship. During this time, any city which managed to have such a temple was highly honored and was given the title *Neocorus*—Temple Warden. Thus, the competition to have such a temple was severe.

History tells us that Ephesus won this title during the reign of four emperors. And thus her pride increased.

When Paul entered the city to stay and establish the church in A.D. 53, he had many human reasons to be discouraged. Besides emperor worship, the worship of Artemis, and a strong Jewish element, the city was drenched in immorality—and was exceedingly superstitious. An inscription on a building proclaimed: "If the bird is flying from right to left, and settles out of sight, good luck will come. But if it lifts up its left wing, then, whether it rises or settles out of sight, misfortune will result."

On a previous trip to Ephesus (Acts 18:18-21), Paul had arrived with his old friends, Priscilla and Aquila. This couple had worked with him in Corinth and were strong in the faith. Thus, when Apollos of Alexandria went to Ephesus and began to preach, this couple gave him doctrinal instruction which he gladly accepted.

Ephesus

Again, Paul started his work in the synagogue where he continued to preach for three months, and then he moved into the lecture hall of Tyrannus where he remained for "the space of two years." And so successful was he, Luke reported: "... all they which dwelt in Asia heard the word of the Lord Jesus, both Jews and Greeks" (Acts 19:10).

In addition to this, the gospel overcame the superstitions of many. Luke wrote: "Many of them also which used curious arts brought their books together, and burned them before all men: and they counted the price of them, and found it fifty thousand pieces of silver" (Acts 19:19; it has been estimated that this was equivalent to $10,000).

All of this success, however, infuriated the silversmiths, for much of their living came from making silver shrines of Artemis. Demetrius was especially incensed. After gathering the silversmiths, he expounded his complaint: "Sirs, ye know that by this craft we have our wealth. Moreover ye see and hear, that not alone at Ephesus, but almost throughout all Asia, this Paul hath persuaded and turned away much people, saying that they be no gods, which are made with hands" (Acts 19:25,26).

Demetrius then whipped up the crowd until the "whole city was filled with confusion" (verse 29). Next, having caught Gaius and Aristarchus, friends of Paul, they rushed them into the great amphitheater—a stadium-like affair that seated 24,500.

Utter confusion followed. Finally, Alexander was helped to the front and he managed to get the mob's attention. But when it became apparent that he was a Jew, the people became hysterical and for two hours they kept repeating as with one voice "Great is Diana of the Ephesians" (verse 34).

Undoubtedly many would have been killed had it not been for the town clerk who miraculously established quiet and then said: "Ye men of Ephesus, what man is there that knoweth not how that the city of the Ephesians is a worshipper of the great goddess Diana, and of the image which fell down from Jupiter? Seeing then that

Ephesus

these things cannot be spoken against, ye ought to be quiet and to do nothing rashly" (Acts 19:35,36).

He next pointed out that they could take the matter to court. This calmed them and "he dismissed the assembly."

Paul, however, felt that the Holy Spirit was directing him to another city, and so after embracing the disciples he left for Macedonia.

Paul's years in Ephesus had been fruitful in spite of some periods of unpleasantness. In his first letter to the Corinthians, he mentioned having "fought with beasts at Ephesus" (15:32). Does this mean Paul was imprisoned in Ephesus? Perhaps! Indeed, there are scholars who think that some of his prison epistles were written in Ephesus. Writing to the Corinthians, Paul said: "For we would not, brethren, have you ignorant of our trouble which came to us in Asia, that we were pressed out of measure, above strength, insomuch that we despaired even of life" (II Corinthians 1:8).

To many, that passage refers to a deeper trouble than was caused by Demetrius at the theater.

Another argument in favor of an imprisonment in Ephesus centers around the slave, Onesimus. Having fled from his master at Colossae (Colossians 4:9), he went to Paul who was in prison to request help. Paul responded to his plea by writing the beautiful letter known as Philemon.

Since Colossae was only one hundred miles east of Ephesus, and Rome was at least one thousand miles west of Colossae, it is reasonable to assume that it would have been more likely that Onesimus would have called on Paul at Ephesus. And this idea is especially significant when we realize that on a trip to Rome, Onesimus would have had to cross two oceans and hundreds of miles of land. True, passports were not required. Still, many embarrassing questions might have been asked, and in Roman times runaway slaves found it almost impossible to escape.

In Acts 20:16,17 we see Paul at Miletus. Here, he had

Ephesus

arranged for the Ephesian elders to come over and see him. But why didn't he stop at Ephesus only a short distance away? Luke tells us: "Paul had determined to sail by Ephesus, because he would not spend the time in Asia: for he hasted, if it were possible for him, to be at Jerusalem the day of Pentecost" (Acts 20:16). That was a good reason. And yet he might have arranged to have reached Miletus a day or two earlier, and then spent some time in Ephesus.

But there is a hint that he wanted to avoid Ephesus. Why? J. T. Wood made the interesting suggestion that perhaps an inscription had been posted on the theater forbidding him to preach there. And it is quite possible that that was at least part of the reason. Paul was a law abiding man!

CHAPTER 8

Antioch

When it concerns the church, Antioch was a city of firsts. It was the first city to have a Gentile congregation. It was the first city to send out missionaries. It was the first city to provide relief for another congregation, and it was the first city in which followers of Christ were sneered at as "Christians."

In addition, the church at Antioch had some of the most colorful experiences recorded in the New Testament. It was here Paul withstood Peter to the face, and it was here the controversy over circumcision stirred to the surface.

Ah, but what Antioch are we writing about? The New Testament speaks of two Antiochs, and history lets us know that there was another fourteen. Sixteen Antiochs existing at the same time and in the same approximate area sounds like an interesting story. And it is! But our concern here is with the Syrian Antioch, the Antioch of this chapter.

When Alexander the Great died in 323 B.C., he died without a will. This meant that his vast empire would go to the strongest. Eventually, Seleucus—one of Alexander's generals—became the ruler of Syria. Burning with a

Antioch

passion to perpetuate the name of his father Antiochus, Seleucus founded and named the sixteen cities after him. Since, however, it was an ancient practice to alternate the name of a family, it is debated whether Seleucus named the city after his father Antiochus or after his son Antiochus.

The approximate site of Antioch was selected by Alexander the Great. At the end of the battle of Issus in which he defeated the Persian king, Darius III, Alexander marched south to Phoenicia where he began his seven-month siege of Tyre. On the way, he paused just east of the city. Here he drank from a spring. And since the water was so refreshing, he impulsively decided to build a city near the spot. But since he was in the midst of planning a new campaign, he merely stayed long enough to order a temple built for Zeus.

Around 300 B.C., Seleucus made a series of sacrifices to the local gods and pled their guidance in founding the city. As the sacrifices were burning, so insists the incredible legend, an eagle—the bird of Zeus—swooped down and snatched a piece of meat from the flaming altar. Seleucus then hurriedly commanded his son to follow the eagle on horseback. The eagle flew to the temple of Zeus and dropped the meat on its altar. Thus convinced of the location, Seleucus asked his architect, Xenarius, to lay out the city.

According to the procedure of the period, army elephants were stationed at the points where the towers in the wall were to be built, and the streets were marked with wheat. "The size of the settlement did not fill the whole site. Seleucus built on the level ground near the river in order to avoid the wash from Mount Silpius. The settlement lay in an oblong shape, between the river and the road that in Roman times became the colonnaded main street. The agora or market place, which is still the industrial and commercial quarter of the modern city, lay along the bank of the river" (Ancient Antioch by Glanville Downey).

The entire city, including the section for Europeans and

Antioch

the one for Syrians, covered less than a square mile. And since New Testament Antioch had a population estimated at around half a million and was second in size only to Rome and Alexandria, this part of the city was a mere nucleus.

Glanville Downey wrote: "... the streets had no relation to the river [Orontes], but were very carefully oriented with respect to the sun and the prevailing winds; they were laid out to take advantage of shade in the summer and sun in the winter, and the direction of the main avenues along the long axis was calculated so as to catch the regular breeze which blew from the sea up the valley of the Orontes in the summer."

And thus Syrian Antioch, located on the bank of the Orontes, at the top of the Fertile Crescent, came into being. With Mount Silpius in the background, the navigable river connected the city to the Mediterranean twenty miles to the front, and with a favorable climate, Antioch was ideally located.

A suburb of Antioch, known for its beauty, came to be so closely associated with Antioch, the two cities were frequently named together. With its cypress trees, Temple of Apollo, fountains, and waterfalls, Daphne became a popular resort. Its popularity grew with the centuries. An Olympic stadium was built there and the Olympic Games of Antioch rivaled those of Greece. Roman emperors and Hellenistic kings liked to spend their summers there. The "park" sported a theater, private baths, expensive villas—and "houses of pleasure." Gradually the worship of Apollo was combined with the worship of Artemis, and this added to the vile reputation of the place for being a cesspool of immorality.

In the middle of the first century B.C., the seacoast around Antioch became a hiding place for pirates. During his assignment to clear the Mediterranean of these privateers, Pompey put Antioch and the rest of Syria under Roman control. He made Antioch the capital of the new province and gave it freedom to manage its own internal affairs.

Antioch

Soon the Romans began to beautify Antioch. They were lavish with colonnades, fountains, public buildings. One of the most famous buildings erected at this time was the basilica of Julius Caesar which he named the Kaisarion—after himself. Part of the ruins of this can still be seen. Roman statues of emperors and gods lined the streets, and an amphitheater was constructed for gladiatorial fights.

When Antioch was jolted by a severe earthquake in A.D. 37, Caligula sent help at once to repair the damage. And having inherited a full treasury from Tiberius, he spent money lavishly. Indeed, he built many new buildings.

While these things were going on, Jesus Christ was crucified outside the gates of Jerusalem some 300 miles to the south. And then following His resurrection, ascension, and the outpouring of the Holy Spirit on the day of Pentecost, the church leaped forward—especially in Jerusalem.

As the church in Jerusalem expanded, deacons were chosen to look after the business affairs of the church. Among the seven chosen was "Nicolas a proselyte of Antioch" (Acts 6:5). All went well until the stoning of Stephen—another of the deacons. Persecutions followed and many of the believers were "scattered abroad."

Some went to Phenice, others to Cyprus, and still others to Antioch. These refugees continued to preach "but unto the Jews only" (Acts 11:19). Others, however, felt that the words of Jesus should also be preached to non-Jews. Some of these men were from Cyprus and Cyrene "which, when they were come to Antioch, spake unto the Grecians, preaching the Lord Jesus" (Acts 11:20). Was Nicolas, the proselyte of Antioch, one of these? We are not told.

This mission to the Greeks in Antioch was so successful Luke wrote: "And the hand of the Lord was with them: and a great number believed, and turned unto the Lord" (Acts 11:21). Among the members of this congregation was Manaen, an intimate friend, and perhaps even the foster-brother of Herod the Tetrarch (Acts 13:1).

The congregation was spiritually well equipped. "Now

Antioch

there were in the church that was at Antioch certain prophets and teachers" (Acts 13:1). Moreover, the leaders in the congregation were Spirit-filled, dedicated men.

When the story of the success of the church at Antioch reached the brethren in Jerusalem, they were delighted. Indeed, they were so delighted, they sent Barnabas to help them. This was an ideal choice for Barnabas was from Cyprus, and thus understood the Greek mind. In addition, he was a Levite and was thus accepted by the Jews.

While at Antioch, Barnabas went to Tarsus—about 150 miles away by land—to find Saul. "And when he had found him, he brought him unto Antioch. And it came to pass, that a whole year they assembled themselves with the church, and taught much people" (Acts 11:26).

Where did Paul and Barnabas preach during this stay? Again, no one knows. But there are two interesting legends, mentioned by Downey. One is that they preached on a street near the Roman Pantheon. This street was called either Singon or Saigon which means "jawbone"!

The other legend, expounded by the "Pseudo-Clementine Romance," written in the first part of the third century, declares that Theophilus—the one to whom Luke addressed his works—donated a "huge" house for the use of the church. These legends like so many others may or may not be true. But even if they are completely false, they do indicate what people have thought.

Up until this time, the word *Christian* had never been used. The followers of Christ had been called *believers, saints, brethren, disciples, those that call upon the name of the Lord,* and other such titles.

And now Acts 11:26 tells us: "And the disciples were called Christians first in Antioch." H. V. Morton has an interesting comment on this in his excellent book, *In the Steps of St. Paul.* "The word could not have been coined by the Jews, because they used the word Nazarene, and it is unlikely that it was applied by the Christians, for they called themselves 'saints,' 'brethren,' and 'believers.' It follows, therefore, that it was probably a word coined by a Greek, who, knowing something about the new faith,

Antioch

incorporated the name of Jesus Christ with those who believed in Him.

"There is further possibility that the word was used disparagingly by the Roman officials at Antioch, just as the followers of Caesar were dubbed Caesarini, of Pompey, Pompeiani, of Herod, Herodiani. If so, we may imagine that the word Christians was possibly first used by a member of the Antioch police force when he was summoned to a street in which Orthodox Jews had attacked the new sect.

"'Those Christiani again!' he may have said, unconscious that he had made history."

During one of the meetings at Antioch, Agabus, a prophet from Jerusalem, stood up and predicted that "there should be great dearth throughout all the world" (Acts 11;28). This prediction came to pass, probably about A.D. 46. A special offering was taken and Paul and Barnabas were selected to deliver the money to Jerusalem. How the money was carried is not known, but it is quite likely that they used a letter of credit, or perhaps a traveler's check.

It is also possible that they took along a letter which explained a disagreement which the church in Antioch was having over the keeping of the law. Some of the Judaizers had contended "Except ye be circumcised after the manner of Moses, ye cannot be saved"(Acts 15:1).

The funds for famine relief were presented, and the problem about Gentiles being required to keep the law of Moses was outlined. Peter, as usual, was quick to speak. He insisted that God had "put no difference between us and them, purifying their hearts by faith. Now therefore why tempt ye God, to put a yoke upon the neck of the disciples, which neither our fathers nor we were able to bear?" (Acts 15:9,10).

The conclusion of the Jerusalem brethren was that the Gentiles should "abstain from pollutions of idols, and from fornication, and from things strangled, and from blood" (Acts 15:20). This verdict was written out and sent to Antioch "and when they had gathered the multitude

Antioch

together, they delivered the epistle: Which when they had read, they rejoiced for the consolation" (Acts 15:30,31).

One would think that this was the end of the matter. But it was not. Paul tells us what happened in his letter to the Galatians. Galatians 2:11-16 records his words as follows: "But when Peter was come to Antioch, I withstood him to the face, because he was to be blamed. For before that certain came from James, he did eat with the Gentiles: but when they were come, he withdrew and separated himself, fearing them which were of the circumcision. And the other Jews dissembled likewise with him; insomuch that Barnabas also was carried away with their dissimulation. But when I saw that they walked not uprightly according to the truth of the gospel, I said unto Peter before them all, If thou, being a Jew, livest after the manner of Gentiles, and not as do the Jews, why compellest thou the Gentiles to live as do the Jews? We who are Jews by nature, and not sinners of the Gentiles, knowing that a man is not justified by the works of the law, but by the faith of Jesus Christ, even we have believed in Jesus Christ, that we might be justified by the faith of Christ, and not by the works of the law: for by the works of the law shall no flesh be justified."

The sharp differences between Paul and Peter and Barnabas and John Mark might have torn the church in Antioch asunder. But all of them were big men and would not allow these differences to either hinder the church or soil their mutual esteem.

It was in Antioch that Paul received his summons to do missionary work. Luke records: "... the Holy Ghost said, Separate me Barnabas and Saul for the work whereunto I have called them. And when they had fasted and prayed, and laid their hands on them, they sent them away" (Acts 13:2,3). And so the first missionary church was born at Antioch!

Considering how the work grew in Antioch, and how refugees from the persecution in Jerusalem fled there, the question arises: Why did these things happen in Antioch? From a merely human point of view, there is a suggested

Antioch

answer. The population of Antioch was perhaps three times that of Jerusalem, and the civil government seemed to have better control over Jewish mobs in Antioch than they did in Jerusalem.

The ultimate answer, of course, is that God had planned it to be this way just as He had planned for Paul to go to Philippi rather than to Bithynia.

Before going to the next chapter, we must say a word about the other Antioch referred to in the New Testament—Pisidian Antioch. This city, north of Perga in the Roman province of Pisidia, was about three hundred miles west of the Syrian Antioch. The town had been well fortified by the Romans in order to keep peace among the neighboring tribes.

Luke tells us that Paul and Barnabas preached there on their first missionary journey (Acts 13:14). And that Paul visited it on his second and third missionary journeys (Acts 16:6 and 18:23). On the first journey, Paul preached in the synagogue, and Luke gives us a detailed account of his sermon (Acts 13:16-41). The result of this sermon was that "the next sabbath day came almost the whole city together to hear the word of God" (Acts 13:44).

This success stirred up a mob and they turned on Paul and Barnabas "and expelled them out of their coasts" (verse 50). After shaking the dust from their feet, Paul and his friend went to Iconium where they had great success and ultimately faced another mob—one that sought to stone them. From here they went to Lystra where they had so much success the crowd wanted to call Barnabas Jupiter and Paul Mercurius. But again, they faced persecution. This time, according to Acts 14:19, "And there came thither certain Jews from Antioch and Iconium who persuaded the people, and, having stoned Paul, drew him out of the city, supposing he had been dead."

Later, Paul ordained elders in Pisidian Antioch and in the neighboring towns (Acts 14:23). Some believe that Paul's letter to the Galatians was partly intended for the church in this city.

CHAPTER 9

Tarsus

My well-illustrated travel book on Turkey is crammed with hotel addresses, descriptions of Istanbul's night life, maps, menus, a money exchange table, and the lure of exotic restaurants; but nowhere in its more than two hundred pages is the city of Tarsus even mentioned. This is a pity, for its illustrious son Paul was certainly one of the half dozen most useful men who ever lived.

The Tarsus where Paul was born between A.D. 10 and 15 was at the time a city of approximately half a million. Today the population has shrunk to a mere 25,000. Nevertheless, to historians and Bible students, Tarsus, like Bethlehem, remains one of the historic cities of the world.

Located near the northeastern end of the Mediterranean, this former city of culture and learning competed with Alexandria and Rome as one of the best cities in the Empire. But had it not been for two famous passes, Tarsus would never have been even a major city.

Except for the southern front which faces the sea, this city of Paul is hedged in by the snarling teeth of two chains of jagged mountains. The snow-tipped peaks of the Taurus range block the northern and western side of Tarsus, while

Tarsus

the Amanus mountains block the eastern side—the side facing Syria.

Many centuries B.C—no one knows exactly how many—engineers chiseled a pass by the side of a riverbed that crosses the Taurus Mountains. This road which Xenophon described as being a "wagon-road, exceedingly steep and impracticable for an army to pass," was about eighty miles long. But the pass, known as the Cilician Gates, is a mere slit. The gates, however, opened the way from Tarsus to the West. On the other side, the Syrian Gates opened the way across the Amanus mountains to the East.

The Cilician Gates have a romantic history probably unequaled by any other pass. It was through them that Cyrus the Younger and his Ten Thousand marched on their way to Babylon in the summer of 401 B.C. And it was through them that Alexander the Great passed on his way to Tarsus in 333 B.C. after his great victory over the Persians on the banks of the Granicus.

When from a distance Alexander viewed the almost impossible-to-believe slit in the mountains, he feared an ambush. Remembering how the Spartans had fought at the pass of Thermopylae, he was reluctant to take a chance. And so he sent his Thracians up to the pass to see if it was protected. To his amazement, the young conqueror learned that the Persians had fled. Alexander then ordered his men forward.

Overheated because of his trek through the pass and down to Tarsus, Alexander plunged into the snow-chilled Cydnus river. Coming out of the water, he developed a sudden high fever. His physician Philip, a student of Hippocrates, mixed a medicine and assured Alexander that if he swallowed it, he could be cured.

But just as Alexander reached for the cup, he was given a frantic letter from Parmenio—one of his generals. The letter declared that Philip was in the pay of Darius and that the medicine was deadly poison. Alexander, however, was desperate. With a quick thrust of his hand he gulped

Tarsus

down the potion and handed the message to Philip.

Alexander lived. But one wonders what would have happened if he had died and the Hellenization of the world had stopped. In that event it is probable that the New Testament would not have been written in Greek!

From Xenophon, the historian who traveled with the Ten Thousand, we have an eyewitness description of Tarsus and the plains surrounding it as it appeared four centuries before the birth of Paul. "Thence he (Cyrus the Younger) descended to a large and beautiful plain, well-watered and full of trees of all sorts and vines; it produces an abundance of sesame, millet, wheat and barley, and it is surrounded on every side from sea to sea, by a lofty and formidable range of mountains. After descending he marched through this plain . . . to Tarsus, a large and prosperous city of Cilicia where the palace of Syennesis, the king of the Cilicians, was situated; and through the middle of the city flows a river named the Cydnus, two plethora in width. [A plethora was 97 feet, hence the river was 194 feet wide.] The inhabitants of this city had abandoned it and fled, with Syennesis, to a stronghold upon the mountains—all of them . . . except the tavern-keepers."

In Paul's time, the city was much the same as Xenophon describes it. Only it was much larger. The Cydnus connected the city to the Mediterranean about ten miles away. As a lad, Paul must have watched the ships move up the river and unload their cargoes at the artificial docks in the midst of the city.

Some forty years before Paul's birth, Cleopatra had sailed up this river in order to meet Mark Antony. Antony had just arrived in the city after celebrating his victory over Brutus and Cassius at Philippi. And now he was annoyed at Cleopatra for having aided Cassius.

Since the Queen of Egypt did not know what awaited her, she decided to use her charms. And on that memorable day, the citizens of Tarsus saw a most unusual sight, and it is entirely possible that Paul's father was

Tarsus

among the witnesses.

With its purple sails spread, its silver oars chunking to the rhythm of harps, flutes, and pipes, and with its gilded stern glistening in the sun, Cleopatra's ship moved majestically up the river. Cleopatra, realizing her peril, did not take chances. Having vast wealth, she used it.

Dressed in the finest silks in order to resemble Aphrodite, the goddess of love, she lounged seductively beneath an awning trimmed with gold. Fabulous jewels shimmered on her throat, wrists, and arms. Her hair, also, was decorated with jewels, and there were jewels on her fingers and hanging from her ears. And on each side of the awning, boys, dressed as cupid, fanned her with the most expensive fans the treasury of Egypt could provide.

Other ships of the fleet followed and in these were the finest entertainers, magicians, and cooks. Cleopatra knew that Antony loved Egyptian cooking and she was prepared to provide it.

Clouds of exquisite perfume were everywhere. As Antony stepped on board he must have known that he was stepping into a spider's web. But like Herod when he was enticed by Salome, he didn't care.

Undoubtedly, Paul heard this story with countless variations dozens of times; and in the years that followed, when he wrote about lust and gluttony, he must have thought about this scene.

About a mile above the city, the Cydnus tumbles over a waterfall composed of large blocks of granite. From the wild currents and mists of these falls the river flows through the city into a small lake six or seven miles below and from thence into the sea.

In Paul's day there was a wealthy suburb just north of Tarsus in the foothills. It was to this suburb that the wealthy fled during the humid summers.

Tarsus was a city of activity—and learning. Timber from the mountains was floated down on the streams and loaded into the ships that were anchored in Tarsus. Also, the city was known for its tent making. Cilician goats'

Tarsus

hair was famous for its durability throughout the world. And this material was used for items other than tents. Perhaps Paul's cloak which he "left at Troas with Carpus" was made of this stiff material.

Rabbis had insinuated that weaving and tanning were not good occupations for Jews; but Tarsus was an independent city, and Paul did not feel bound by this prejudice. Tradition tells us that his father was a cloth merchant and a dealer in tents. Also, we are reminded of the fact that Paul, a tentmaker, was not ashamed to associate with others in the same trade—Aquila and Priscilla for example.

Tarsus was a unique crossroads of the East and the West. It had little if any anti-Semitism, and race prejudice was at a low minimum. This unique background served to help Paul develop his broad world outlook. Morally, Tarsus was a rather conservative city. In other cities, especially in Ionia, the women walked the streets in rather scanty clothes. Not so in Tarsus. Here, perhaps influenced by the Persians, the women wore veils on the streets. Some think that Paul was influenced by this custom when he wrote that a woman should wear a covering on her head as a sign that she is under man's authority (I Corinthians 11:10).

Learning in Tarsus was both a passion and a pride. Like other cities in the Empire, it had a state-supported university. Writing about this, Strabo pointed out that unlike other universities whose student body came mostly from abroad, the university in Tarsus was filled with Cilician students. Indeed, he declared that the passion to learn in Tarsus was higher than in either Athens or Alexandria.

One of the distinguished citizens of Tarsus was the Stoic philosopher Athenodorus who had passed away a decade or two before Paul's birth. He had lectured all over the world, and one of his students was Augustus Caesar. Before leaving for Athens, he had a word of caution for the Emperor. "Whenever you get angry do not say or do

Tarsus

anything before repeating to yourself the twenty-four letters of the alphabet."

Augustus was so pleased with this advice, he invited the old man to remain with him for another year!

It was in Tarsus that Paul, or Saul as he was known in his native city, went to school. Here, he studied the Law, learned Hebrew, and was drilled in all the strictness taught by the Pharisees. Day after day, he was taught, "Don't do this! Avoid that! That is wrong! Keep the Law!"

He was probably taught to avoid Gentile learning, art, and literature. But Tarsus was such a cosmopolitan city, these things could not be completely avoided. When asked to identify himself, Paul said to the chief captain, "I am a man which am a Jew of Tarsus, a city in Cilicia, a citizen of no mean city" (Acts 21:39). In this we find an echo of the famous Greek playwright Euripides.

Paul was, of course, a Roman citizen. This citzenship was his by birth, for his parents were also citizens. Frequently in his day, high-class Jews purchased this citizenship. The price was a minimum of five hundred drachmas.

At the proper age, probably thirteen, Paul was sent to Jerusalem to study under Gamaliel—grandson of the well known Hillel. Following his conversion to Christ, Paul eventually returned to Tarsus (Acts 9:30). Here, he worked in comparative obscurity for an estimated ten years. It was while he was in Tarsus that Barnabas summoned him to help in the work at Antioch (Acts 11:25,26).

In modern Tarsus, a guide will point to a rocky cavern and claim that this is where Paul lived as a hermit during this period of waiting. But since Paul was always an active man, this is hard to accept. It is more likely that he returned to his trade, preached, and searched the Scriptures. Galatians 1:21-23 hints that during this time he did some evangelistic work.

CHAPTER 10

Jericho

The city of Jericho has a dozen meanings to a dozen groups—all of them different, and yet all of them romantic!

On driving into the war-scarred city, a Christian is apt to think of little Zacchaeus and the sycamore tree; an Arab might remember the day when it was an Arab stronghold; an orthodox Jew's mind would probably go back to Joshua; and an archaeologist would undoubtedly smile, considering the important discoveries made there.

Fortunately for scholars, the present Jericho is some distance from both the New Testament and the Old Testament Jericho. This means that archaeologists have been free to dig without complaints that they were ruining someone's backyard. And today a number of eminent archaeologists claim that ancient Jericho was the oldest city in the world, and that it was the lowest city on earth.

Some scholars believe that the original Jericho dates back a minimum of 5,000 years before Christ. If this date is correct, the area was inhabited at least 3,500 years before Joshua appeared on the scene!

Crouched in the scorching desert, 900 feet below sea

Jericho

The lovely city of Jericho is alive with palms and flowers, history, and sorrow. This picture taken by the author in 1970 shows a shell hole in the road sign. When asked, an Arab said the shelling had taken place about two months previously.

Jericho

level—(Death Valley is only 276 feet below)—and six miles northwest of the northern end of the Dead Sea, the city has a warm, humid climate.

Palm-studded Jericho—the name means place of fragrance or moon city—has retained much of its original character throughout the centuries. When Moses viewed it from Mount Nebo, he referred to it as "the city of palm trees" (Deuteronomy 34:3).

Since Jericho, on a straight line from Jerusalem, is a mere seventeen miles away, those seeking an abrupt change from Jerusalem's 2,550-foot altitude, slip down to Jericho just as people have done for thousands of years. This contrasting climate has made Jericho a valuable tourist attraction from its beginning.

The city has an excellent water supply and the soil is extremely fertile. In addition to these assets, the background hills rise to an altitude of 1,500 feet, thus supplying excellent protection from an invader. Today, as one stands in the city and views these hills, he is reminded of the words of Rahab, spoken to the spies she had concealed. "And she said unto them, Get you to the mountain, lest the pursuers meet you; and hide yourselves there three days, until the pursuers be returned: and afterward may ye go your way" (Joshua 2:16).

It was on one of these hills, Quarantania, just west of the city, that tradition says Jesus was tempted by Satan.

The mound that now rises over the Old Testament Jericho is known as Tell es-Sultan. Since several cities are believed to have been built and then destroyed in this general area, scientists have named them City A, and City B, and so on.

According to John Garstang, the British archaeologist who worked on the Jericho project from 1930 to 1936, the "late bronze age city"— the one destroyed by Joshua—was city D. Other scientists had already concluded that this ancient city was surrounded by two walls: an outer wall six feet thick and an inner wall twelve feet thick. The outer wall was estimated to have been from

Jericho

twenty-five to thirty feet high.

Also, a number of archaeologists were certain there was evidence that houses had been built on the inner wall. This conclusion would agree with Scripture, for Joshua 2:15 reads: "Then she let them down by a cord through the window: for her house was upon the town wall, and she dwelt upon the wall."

Garstang startled the Christian world by declaring: "The space between the two walls is filled with fragments and rubble. There are clear traces of a tremendous fire, compact masses of blackened bricks, cracked stones, charred wood, and ashes. All along the walls the houses have been burned to the ground and their roofs have crashed on top of them."

Again, we have agreement with Scripture. "... and the people shouted with a great shout, [and] ... the wall fell down flat ... And they burnt the city with fire, and all that was therein" (Joshua 6:20,24).

Many have wondered how Joshua could have marched his men around the city wall in a single day. But archaeological studies show that this was entirely possible, for the complete city covered an area of only about eight acres: the size of a large mobile-home court.

The terror of the occupants of Jericho must have reached fever pitch as they watched the silent army with its priests and ark solemnly marching around the city. Their whispered conversations are reflected in what Rahab had said to the spies. "And she said unto the men, I know that the Lord hath given you the land, and that your terror is fallen upon us, and that all the inhabitants of the land faint because of you. For we have heard how the Lord dried up the water of the Red Sea for you, when ye came out of Egypt.... And as soon as we had heard these things, our hearts did melt, neither did there remain any more courage in any man, because of you: for the Lord your God, he is God in heaven above, and in earth beneath" (Joshua 2:9-11).

Following Garstang's work, Miss Kathleen Kenyon

Jericho

The Jericho area is now governed by Israel. This photo shows an agricultural station operated by the Israelis to help the Arab population make better use of the soil.

Jericho

went to Jericho in 1952 and began to excavate. Dr. John B. Graybill, writing in the *Zondervan Pictorial Bible Dictionary* (1963), has this to say about her findings: "After seven seasons at Jericho, Miss Kenyon reports that virtually nothing remains of the Jericho of the period of Joshua (1500-1200 B.C.). The mound has suffered such denudation that almost all remains later than the third millenium B.C. have disappeared. The two walls which Garstang connected with his city D Miss Kenyon discovered to date from the third millennium, hundreds of years before the Exodus. Only a bit of pottery and possibly one building remain from the late bronze age .... Many scholars now believe that the Jericho of Joshua's day was little more than a fort."

The part of the building and the bit of pottery that Miss Kenyon did find, however, is of great interest. Near an ancient type oven—similar to those used by Palestinian peasants today—standing like a topless cone in the middle of the floor, there is a little jug. This bit of pottery has been dated about 1400 B.C. Concerning this, Miss Kenyon remarked, in her *Digging Up Jericho*: "The evidence seems to me to be that the small fragment of a building that we have found is part of the kitchen of a Canaanite woman, who may have dropped the juglet beside the oven and fled at the sound of the trumpets of Joshua's men."

Archaeologists are agreed that the walls fell because of an earthquake. But even though earthquakes are credited with felling the walls and damming up the Jordan, we must remember that these events happened at precisely the right time, and thus we must acknowledge the Divine intervention.

Having taken Jericho, Joshua made a solemn prophecy. "Cursed be the man before the Lord, that riseth up and buildeth this city Jericho: he shall lay the foundation thereof in his firstborn, and in his youngest son shall he set up the gates of it" (Joshua 6:26).

This prediction proved to be remarkably accurate. No one attempted to build on the ruins until the time of

Jericho

Ahab—some five or six hundred years later. Then Hiel attempted to do just that. The story of the subsequent disaster is noted in I Kings 16:34. Matthew Henry wrote: "He began to build in defiance of the curse well known in Israel, jesting with it perhaps as a bugbear.... He built for his children, but God wrote him childless; his eldest son died when he began, and the youngest when he finished, and all the rest (it is supposed) in between."

New Testament Jericho has never drawn the interest that has settled on the old city. Serious excavations did not start until 1950. But the site is of great interest; for because of the city's warm climate, the new city became a favorite place for those in power.

Mark Antony presented Jericho to Cleopatra; and she, in turn, rented it to Herod the Great for a reported annual rental of $150,000. Herod had a winter palace there, and the Romans saw to it that the city was equipped with those luxuries they considered essential to the "good life." Thus, there were elaborate baths, wine cellars, vast floors tiled with mosaic, huge pictures, lively gardens, fountains, and many elaborate buildings.

It was here that Herod the Great died in 4 B.C.

Following the Moslem conquest of Palestine, Caliph Hisham Ibn Abdul built a magnificent palace for himself just north of the present Jericho. Like Herod, he loved the climate and decided on a breath-taking palace. There were enormous mosaic floors, exquisite gardens, elaborately carved fountains, rows of high, fluted columns, and fantastic pictures covering entire walls. But just as this structure—known as the Omayyad Palace—was being completed in A.D. 747, an earthquake shook it down and it has never been rebuilt.

Today visitors flock to see the ruins, but there is not much left except for some floors and the remains of some walls. Many of the ornaments and decorations can now be seen in the Rockefeller Museum in Jerusalem.

During my visit in 1958, Jericho was still in the hands of the Jordanians. But since the Six-Day War it has been

Jericho

governed by Israel. On my next tour in 1970, I found that the Israelis were operating an agricultural station there in order to help the Arab population make better use of the soil. Tiring of the lecture being given to us beneath the palm trees, I went out to the street. There I found that a shell had recently passed through the road sign.

When I asked an Arab about it, he said the shelling had taken place about two months before.

The lovely city of Jericho is alive with flowers, history—and sorrow. The spring of Elisha still bubbles in the center of the town. As one views it, he thinks of its intriguing history as recorded in 11 Kings 2:21-22. Finding the spring bitter, Elisha prayed for guidance and then "... went forth unto the spring of the waters, and cast the salt in there, and said, Thus saith the Lord, I have healed these waters; there shall not be from thence any more death or barren land. So the waters were healed unto this day...."

In the days of Jesus, Galileans making a pilgrimage to Jerusalem often went through Peraea on the east side of the Jordan in order to avoid Samaria. Those who did this, crossed over the Jordan to Jericho and from thence went to Jerusalem.

Jesus frequently visited Jericho, and while there performed a number of noted miracles. We also remember his famous parable about the man who was beaten and robbed by thieves while on his way to Jericho. The inn where the victim was placed by the Good Samaritan is still pointed out by guides as the tour buses follow the coiling road from Jerusalem down to Jericho.

CHAPTER 11

Bethlehem

As the Christmas season approaches, people all over the world think of Bethlehem—and especially the Christ-child. They remember the church dramas of their youth, the Christmas tree emerging from stacks of gifts and decorated with tinsel and lights, special offerings for missions, and the delightful legends of an ever-plump Santa Claus.

But what we usually forget, or never knew about Bethlehem, is that it is an ancient city with many a key role in history, and that it is also surrounded by an area that bristles with world-shaping events.

Yes, Jesus was born there. But although His birth was the most significant event in the little town's history, there were many other events which are also significant. So let us leave our comfortable room in Jerusalem and go both *down* and *up* to Bethlehem.

We go down, for Bethlehem is just a little over five miles almost due south from Jerusalem; and we go up, for Bethlehem is slightly higher than Jerusalem. All of Bethlehem, however, does not have the same height. The city rests on a limestone ridge and forms a modified semi-

Bethlehem

In Nativity Square in Bethlehem visitors, seen in the distance, await their turn to stoop and enter the low door to the Church of the Nativity built over the traditional place where Jesus was born.

Bethlehem

circle with each end a shade higher than the center. The Church of the Nativity, which commemorates the place where Christ was born, and whose lead roof was once melted to make bullets, stands like a medieval fortress on the southern end of this semicircle.

Reaching out from Bethlehem, like spokes from a hub, are many historical places just a few miles away. Approximately ten miles to the north and a little to the west are the ruins of the ancient city of Gibeon. It was here that Joshua asked the Lord to cause the sun and the moon to stand still (Joshua 10:12-14). And a mere twelve miles almost due west is the sight of Socoh where David confronted Goliath (I Samuel 17). Then if we go six miles to the southeast we come to the birthplace of Amos of Tekoa (Amos 1:1). And three or four miles northwest of Tekoa are the ruins of Herodium. This is the place where Herod the Great stopped the Parthians who were pursuing him from Jerusalem. Herod built a fort here, and it is also the place of his burial.

Next, by dropping fifteen miles almost due south we come to Hebron, the still-thriving city where Abraham's wife Sarah died (Genesis 23:2).

Bethlehem, sometimes referred to in the King James Version as Bethlehem-judah in order to distinguish it from another town by the same name in Zebulun, gets its name from a Hebrew and Aramaic word which means "house of bread." Today, the Arabs call it Beit Lahm, which means "house of meat."

The city is old—and distinguished. In the Bible it is first mentioned in Genesis 35:19—"And Rachel died, and was buried in the way to Ephrath, which is Beth-lehem." The Ephrath here—a variation of Ephrata, etc.—means "fruitful." Rachel's tomb can be seen today just north of Bethlehem on the way to Jerusalem.

The first reference to Bethlehem in the secular world is found in the Armana letters. These letters—discovered in 1887 at El-Armana, 190 miles south of Cairo—are from the diplomatic correspondence between Egypt and other nations. In one of these dispatches, dated by experts to the

Bethlehem

fourteenth century B.C., it is mentioned that Bethlehem belonged to the district of "Urusalim"—Jerusalem.

Thus we have evidence that Bethlehem was flourishing well over three thousand years ago!

Christians like to remember that Bethlehem was the hometown of Boaz whose romance with Ruth is described in the Biblical book by that name. It was their son Obed who became the father of Jesse and the grandfather of David. David grew up in the neighborhood of Bethlehem; and it was in this area that he tended his father's sheep, fought the wild animals, and was eventually anointed King of Israel by the prophet Samuel. And because of this, Luke referred to the place as "the city of David, which is called Bethlehem" (Luke 2:4).

David loved the city, the surrounding Judean hills, the deep well—and the history. One has a feeling that this area is the background for the Twenty-third Psalm. And just as childhood memories bind all of us, they bound David. When Bethlehem fell temporarily under the control of a Philistine garrison, David began to remember the cool water that he used to drink at home. "Oh that one would give me drink of the water of the well of Bethlehem, that is at the gate!" he exclaimed (I Chronicles 11:17).

Impulsively, three brave men broke through the Philistine lines and brought him a drink from the well. But since they had risked their lives, David refused to drink it. Instead, "he poured it out to the Lord."

Following these events and others, Rehoboam—son of Solomon—had the city fortified in the tenth century B.C. This was done to guard the approaches to Jerusalem. He also ordered a food depot to be made there and placed the city under the command of a captain.

Some three centuries later, Micah prophesied, "But thou, Bethlehem Ephratah, though thou be little among the thousands of Judah, yet out of thee shall he come forth unto me that is to be ruler in Israel; whose goings forth have been from of old, from everlasting" (Micah 5:2).

Our next Biblical mention of Bethlehem comes from Ezra who made a listing of those who returned from the

Bethlehem

sixth century B.C. exile in Babylon. Among these, he tells us, were "an hundred twenty and three" from Bethlehem (Ezra 2:21).

The lights of Bethlehem continued to glow during succeeding centuries. The hills remained alive with sheep. Rulers came, left their marks—and were gone. There were abundant harvests, and there were occasional famines.

Then, sometime near 40 B.C., Herod the Great temporarily checked the Parthians a few miles away from the city as we have previously noted.

Thirty some years after that event—no one knows exactly how many—Joseph and Mary made the long sixty-five mile journey from Nazareth to Bethlehem because of "a decree from Caesar Augustus, that all the world should be taxed" (Luke 2:1). (Some scholars render *taxed* as "registered" or "counted.")

It was in Bethlehem that Jesus was born and laid in "a manger; because there was no room for them in the inn" (Luke 2:7). And it was here that the wise men came (Matthew 2:1-11).

Thus the prophecies of Micah, Isaiah, and many others were fulfilled. God had pinpointed Bethlehem to be the place where His only begotten Son would be born, and His will was accomplished.

But Bethlehem was still to remain in the current news.

Alarmed at the inquiries from the wise men about the birth of the King of the Jews, Herod gathered all the chief priests and scribes together and demanded where this one should be born. They quoted for him the prophecy from Micah. The place was Bethlehem. Perhaps remembering his previous struggle near Bethlehem, Herod decided to kill the new-born king at once. Matthew tells us that Herod "slew all the children that were in Bethlehem, and in all the coasts thereof, from two years old and under" (Matthew 2:16).

As far as we know, no church or shrine was built over the traditional "manger" until Constantine built the Church of the Nativity in the first part of the fourth century A.D. But how was he to know the actual spot where Jesus was

Bethlehem

Descending steep stairs in the church to visit the "stable cave," the modern visitor is surprised to find a marble floor and a silver star marking the place—"Here Jesus Christ was born of the Virgin Mary." Low-hung ornate lamps are a part of the ritualistic worship conducted there.

Bethlehem

born? Accurate records were not kept in those days.

Constantine found a way. After the Roman Emperor Hadrian (A.D. 76-138) rebuilt Jerusalem and changed its name to Aelia Capitolina, he systematically destroyed the places venerated by Christians. Over what he believed to be Golgotha, he built a temple to Venus. Over the stable in Bethlehem he built a temple to Adonis—the handsome youth of Greek mythology who, according to Roman legend, fell in love with the goddess Aphrodite. With the place of Christ's birth thus marked, Constantine tore down the pagan building and replaced it with a church.

At various times there were at least three doors to this Church of the Nativity built at the same spot. Now there is only one and it is extremely low. As I stood outside to take a picture, I heard the guide warn, "Don't bump your head." Nevertheless, three people in a row did just that as they entered. The reason for the low entrance is not so that people will have to bow their heads in homage as they enter, as some have assumed. No, it is for a more practical reason than that.

During the many feuds that have scarred Bible lands, there were times when enemies of Christ rode right into the building on horses and donkeys in order to disturb the worshipers. Now such disturbance is impossible. Evidence of two previous doorways can still be seen.

Within a century or two after the construction of the Church of the nativity, it was almost completely destroyed. But it was rebuilt by the Christian emperor Justinian in the Sixth century. One guide assured me that the sturdy Corinthian pillars of dull red stone in the present building are those of Constantine. Some even insist that a few of the pillars were rescued from Hadrian's temple.

In the fifteenth century, decades before Columbus lifted his anchors, King Edward IV of England donated a new roof for the church. The English oak beams and several tons of lead were sent in care of Venetian shippers. They unloaded these supplies at the port of Jaffa—the Biblical Joppa from which Jonah sailed.

Bethlehem

How long these beams stayed in place, no one knows. But it is said that the roof was melted down by the Turks and turned into bullets for use in their war against the Venetians.

The most interesting spot in the building is the stable. However, stables in Palestine in the days of Jesus were not separate building as one might suppose. Instead, the stable—often a cave—was connected to the inn for the convenience of travelers arriving with animals. To reach the stable cave at Bethlehem one must descend two flights of stairs in the church. And there, behind a curtain fringing the top of the cave is a silver star imbedded in marble. Around this star is the inscription *Hic de Virgine Maria Jesus Christus Natus Est*—"Here Jesus Christ was born of the Virgin Mary."

A little over one hundred years ago this star was removed, and the removal led to a quarrel between France and Russia that finally escalated into the Crimean War where may thousands were killed.

It was here that Jerome made his remarkable translation work which ultimately became the Vulgate—a translation of the Bible that is still used by the Roman Catholic Church. The place where he worked is now a wing of the church. Nearby is an altar erected in honor of the "Holy Innocents"—the children killed by the order of Herod in his attempt to kill Jesus.

Bethlehem is no longer the "little town" Philips Brooks visited. This city of David has become the triple town of Bethlehem-Beit Jala Sahur and has a combined population in excess of 27,000, of which 14,400 are nominal Christians. The rest are Moslem. In Bethlehem alone, however, Christians are slightly outnumbered by Moslems.

While walking around Bethlehem, one is apt to see a number of blue eyes. The reason? Simple. There was a time centuries ago when the city overflowed with Crusaders. Ah, but that's another story.

CHAPTER 12

Jerusalem

The information available about Jerusalem is utterly enormous—and easily accessible. According to the Talmud, "When the world was created, it received ten measures of beauty. Nine fell on Jerusalem ... one on the rest of the earth." Thus, to deal with any single aspect, one would require an entire volume.

Since this is the case, we will not write about the city's colorful beginnings, its complex changes across the centuries, nor the many times it has been destroyed. Instead, we shall write about the tomb of Christ and the Temple—now replaced by the Dome of the Rock. Curiously, much of this material is unknown to evangelical Christians. And this is a pity, for these places are visited by millions every year.

While in Jerusalem on vacation from his campaigns in China, General Charles Gordon was directed by a guide to the Church of the Holy Sepulcher—the alleged burial place and the site of the crucifixion of Jesus Christ. Gordon listened with qualified interest as the eager guide explained the story of the church. It seemed that until the year A.D. 325, neither the site of the empty tomb nor the

Jerusalem

crucifixion of Jesus had been located. During that year Bishop Macarius of Jerusalem attended the Council of Nicea. While there, he mentioned this fact to Constantine and suggested that the historic spot was probably under Hadrian's Temple of Venus.

Constantine ordered Macarius to have the temple removed and to make a search. This was done in A.D. 326. The empty tomb, according to the story, and there are many variations, was found beneath the debris. Excited by this discovery, Constantine decreed that a place of prayer be erected on the spot that would "be worthy of the most wonderful place in the world."

Forthwith, the Church of the Holy Sepulcher was built of stone. This building was destroyed and rebuilt several times during the following fifteen hundred years. Still, it is seriously claimed that a certain portion of it remains a part of the original church. But as Gordon viewed the shrine in 1883, he was vaguely dissatisfied. Perhaps some of this uneasiness was because of the amount of gold that had been used in order to "make it worthy." Most of all, however, he was unhappy because the Church of the Holy Sepulcher stands *within* the present walls of Jerusalem, while Hebrews 13:12 states that he "suffered *without* the gate."

Having almost a year of free time to spend in Jerusalem, Gordon began to search for a more suitable site. General Gordon, commonly called Chinese Gordon, was one of the most colorful men who ever lived. He distinguished himself in China where he helped to take Peking, fought in many other parts of the world, and served as Governor of the Sudan. He was an extremely eccentric person, and his eccentricities took many forms. In China, he insisted that his salary be reduced from £3,200 per year to £1,200 per year, and he spent 80 per cent of this on medicines and comforts for his men. When the Prince of Wales invited him for lunch, he refused the invitation on grounds that he went to bed at 9:30! But he got things done, and all of England knew it.

Jerusalem

The Church of the Holy Sepulcher stands over the place Constantine declared was the empty tomb and, vaguely, the place where Christ died on the cross. General Gordon discovered, in 1883, this cliff just outside the Damascus gate that bears a resemblance to a skull. An Arab cemetery is now on top of the hill.

Jerusalem

With Bible in hand, Gordon searched all around Jerusalem for a probable spot that could be identified with the crucifixion. He was wearying from this search when suddenly he noticed a cream-colored cliff from his hotel window. As he studied the wall-like bluff, two hollow eyes and then a portion of a nose seemed to leap out at him. A moment later, it seemed that he was staring at a skull. Leafing quickly to Mark 15:22, he read: "And they bring him unto the place Golgotha, which is, being interpreted, The place of a skull."

Excitedly, he hurried over to the cliff and studied some more. The cliff, he noticed, was just outside the Damascus Gate. This agreed with the passage in Hebrews. Then in John 19:41 he read: "Now in the place where he was crucified there was a garden; and in the garden a new sepulchre, wherein was never man yet laid." This clearly meant that if the cliff was the authentic place there would be an ancient tomb nearby. Gordon went to work immediately. Soon he located a tomb that had been discovered by a Greek in 1867. The tomb was only a few yards from those haunting eyes!

But again he insisted on checking with the New Testament. This time he was fascinated with Mark 15:40: "There were also women looking on afar off . . . ." Thinking of the crowds that watched the crucifixion, and remembering women are usually shorter than men, he decided that if they had seen him from "afar off" the cross would have had to have been on an elevated place.

This reasoning quickened his pulse a trifle more.

Next, he began to question local people. From them he learned that there was a widely circulated legend that in ancient times criminals were frequently tossed to their deaths from those cliffs. He also learned that local Arabs called the place El-Heidemiyeh—The Rent. Thoughts of the rent reminded him of the earthquake that shook the land during the crucifixion.

Thoroughly convinced that he had found the actual place, Gordon drew detailed sketches and mailed them to

Jerusalem

Sir John E. Cowell, Controller of the Household of Buckingham Palace. Soon, interested people united and made an appeal through the *Times* for two thousand pounds with which to purchase the land containing the tomb.

The funds were raised and the land was secured. But is the place authentic? No one really knows, and serious doubts are beginning to emerge. Excavations in Jerusalem by Miss Kathleen Kenyon in 1963 indicate the possibility of another wall. This Second Wall—mentioned by Josephus—may have placed the land occupied by the Church of the Holy Sepulcher *outside* the walls. Moreover, it is quite unreasonable to assume that Bishop Macarius did not know the passage in Hebrews which says that "he suffered without the gate."

Others, however, strongly believe that the cream-colored cliff is the authentic place. Lord Elton, Gordon's biographer, wrote, in *Gordon of Khartoum:* "Gordon was not quite the first to maintain that the Skull Hill . . . was the true site of the crucifixion; at least four writers before Gordon, among them Renan in his *Vie de Jesus,* had championed the theory. But it was the knowledge that it had been endorsed by Gordon which first gained it wide acceptance in Britain and North America."

Rider Haggard, a distinguished novelist whose life covered the period of "discovery," wrote: "Now as it chances, on the cliff at this spot, believed to be the Place of Stoning, and by many that of the crucifixion, the face of the rock, looking toward Jerusalem, has undoubtedly a fantastic, but, to my fancy, a very real resemblance to a rotting human skull . . . .

"There is the low corroded forehead; there are two deep hollows, that make the eyes; there is something which might be the remnant of a nose, and beneath, near to the ground level, a suggestion of twisted and decaying lips . . . . If two thousand years ago, the face of the cliff was approximately as it appears today, may not some fanciful-minded Jews have caught this likeness and designated it on that

Jerusalem

Near the place of the skull, Gordon found a tomb in a former garden area. Today Christians love to visit this Garden Tomb tended by Christians. The photo shows Dr. and Mrs. S. J. Mattar, keepers of the tomb until Dr. Mattar was killed there during the Six Day War.

Jerusalem

account, 'The Place of a Skull'? If so, in view of its traditions and horrible use, the name would have been likely to cling to the site from age to age."

The first time I visited the Garden Tomb—the new name for Gordon's Calvary—it was being kept by Dr. S. J. Mattar, an Arab refugee. Slightly bald, and with a trim moustache, he was garbed in casual western clothes. He and his wife invited me to dinner; and while I waited he showed me around. A thorough Christian, he was one of the most gentle men I have ever met. Unfortunately, during the Six Day War, while he and his wife were hiding in the Empty Tomb, he decided to make a dash for his house to get something. Just outside the Tomb, he was cut down by a trigger-happy Israeli soldier.

The lovely garden of that day has since been improved. Today there are exquisite walks, stone bridges, and benches placed in strategic places for the thousands of tourists who come to meditate and to pray. Many flowers mentioned in the Bible have been planted. There are low hedges of rosemary, brilliant patches of geraniums, tall, shady pines, and large fields of carefully tended grass.

As the years go by, more and more people fall in love with the place, and more and more things show up to increase one's belief in the garden's authenticity. For example, some years ago a number of distinguished archaeologists were asked to examine the tomb. After considerable study, they agreed that it dates back to the time of Herod the Great.

Then in 1952, the keepers began to have trouble with the cistern. While it was being repaired, the workers discovered that it was much larger than it had been previously supposed. Indeed, it was 56 by 33 feet and the distance from the floor to the ceiling was 36 feet—making it a rather large cistern. In addition to the startling size, a cross was found embedded in one of the walls and secured with Roman cement. This could indicate that the place had been used by a congregation for Christian worship. Could it be that this spot was chosen because of its prox-

Jerusalem

imity to the Garden Tomb? Perhaps!

And even more recently, a winepress was found near the tomb. Such a press might indicate that the garden was a flower garden used by a wealthy person such as Joseph of Arimathea who allowed the body of Jesus to be placed in his own personal tomb. It also reminds us of the prophetic words of Isaiah: "I have trodden the winepress alone" (Isaiah 63:3).

Authentic or not, the Garden Tomb is the "must" of all visitors in Jerusalem; and although I have been there several times, when I return to Jerusalem, that is the first place I plan to visit.

To the average tourist the second most interesting place in Jerusalem is the Dome of the Rock, incorrectly called the Mosque of Omar. As Christians advance toward this mosque on the eastern end of the Street of the Chain, many are reminded of the words of Jesus: "And Jesus went out, and departed from the temple: and his disciples came to him for to show him the buildings of the temple. And Jesus said unto them, See ye not all these things? verily I say unto you, There shall not be left here one stone upon another, that shall not be thrown down" (Matthew 24:1,2).

At the time of this conversation, the new temple—commonly called Herod's Temple—started in 20-19 B.C., was only in the midst of construction. Indeed, it was not finished until A.D. 64—a quarter of a century after the crucifixion of Jesus! And even at that time there was some finishing work which the builders planned to do.

Altogether, Herod's Temple occupied approximately twenty-six acres. Upon viewing it, Josephus was overwhelmed. He wrote: "It is the most prodigious work that was ever heard of by man."

But the building the tourist sees is not this one; for, just as Jesus had prophesied, in A.D. 70 Herod's Temple was destroyed and it was never rebuilt. And the fact that it was not rebuilt is quite remarkable, for the Roman emperor, known as Julian the Apostate, determined to do just that. Edward Gibbon wrote: "The restoration of the Jewish

Jerusalem

temple was secretly connected with the ruin of the Christian church." Julian's efforts were frustrated by "an earthquake, a whirlwind, and a fiery eruption." (See *The Decline and Fall of the Roman Empire.)*

After Titus had destroyed Jerusalem, the city remained in ruins. And then, incensed by the Jews, Hadrian completely destroyed the city in A.D. 135. He even ordered the ruins to be obliterated. After this was done, he rebuilt the city on Roman lines and named it Aelia Capitolina. In addition, he decreed that no Jew could enter the city except on special occasions. Violaters were crucified. However, Christians were allowed to remain.

From this time on until A.D. 635 the site of the Temple remained desolate. And remembering the prophecy of Jesus, many Christians rejoiced. Also, they decided to see to it that the Temple was never rebuilt. In their campaign to do this, they piled sewage over the rubble. This thought spread throughout the Empire; and pious Christians, hoping to further the obliteration of the Temple, brought their refuse from as far away as Constantinople! Thus, Mount Moriah became a dunghill.

The only part of the Temple that was not destroyed was a western retaining wall, now popularly known as the Wailing Wall. This Western Wall—the name preferred by the Israelis—attracts Jews from all over the world. The stones in the wall date back to Herod. Today, Jews stand before these massive stones while they read favorite passages from the Old Testament and offer up prayers. In addition, they write out prayers and wedge them between the stones. As they pray, they remember how the power of the Lord filled the Temple after it had been completed by Solomon. "And it came to pass, when the priests were come out of the holy place, that the cloud filled the house of the Lord, so that the priests could not stand to minister because of the cloud: for the glory of the Lord had filled the house of the Lord" (I Kings 8:10, 11).

But Solomon's magnificent Temple lasted for less than four hundred years. It was burned in 587 B.C. by

Jerusalem

Nebuzaradan—Nebuchadnezzar's general—eleven years after King Jehoiachin had been taken captive to Babylon.

The next Temple was built in 516 B.C. and is known as Zerubbabel's Temple. Because of this, one would think that Herod's Temple was the third one. But Jews insist that Herod merely rebuilt and enlarged Zerubbabel's Temple, and that his—the last one—was the Second Temple!

Let us, however, forget the Temple for a moment and step into the Dome of the Rock. Inside, we meet Christians, Moslems, and Jews, for all of these groups have a common heritage in the place. The first thing that takes our attention is the huge bare rock with a hole piercing its center. It is firmly claimed that on this rock—Moriah—that Abraham planned to sacrifice his son Isaac. Moslems also insist that at one time the Ark of the Covenant rested on it, and that it was on this stone that Mohammed mounted his mare el-Burak and made his "Night-Journey" to heaven. According to Moslem legend, this horse had eagle wings, a man's head, and a human voice.

To Christians, the whole area is important, for Jesus often frequented the Temple and taught many a lesson there. Also, when the people took stones to throw at Him, "Jesus hid himself, and went out of the temple, going through the midst of them, and so passed by" (John 8:59).

But the fact that this place is a mosque rather than a church or a temple, plunges us into history again. Up until Jerusalem fell to the Moslems, the whole Temple area was desolate. After the fall, Patriarch Sophronius, the one who represented Jerusalem, met the conquering general, Caliph Omar, on the Mount of Olives in order to arrange terms.

"Verily, you are assured," said Omar, "of the complete security of your lives, your goods, and your churches, which will not be inhabited nor destroyed by Moslems." Following this promise, he dressed in rags and followed Sophronius back to Jerusalem. Soon it was time for Moslems to pray. The Patriarch took him to the church of

Jerusalem

the Holy Sepulcher. But Omar refused to pray there.

"If I had prayed inside the church thou wouldst have lost it," he said. "The believers would have taken it from thee, saying 'Omar prayed here.' " And this undoubtedly was true, for Omar was Islam's second caliph, having followed no other than Abu Bakr, Mohammed's father-in-law!

Sophronius took him to various churches but he would have nothing to do with them. Finally, he led the way to the ancient Temple area and showed Omar the location of the rock known as Moriah. Delighted, Omar ceremoniously cleared away some of the dung with his own hands. After the stone had been cleared by workers, he had a wooden mosque built over it.

Jerusalem was now a Moslem city and its name was changed to El-Kuds (The Holy). El-Kuds was then considered the third most sacred city in Islam, Mecca being first and Medina second. For an entire generation Omar's wooden building seemed to satisfy the people. But in A.D. 687, Mecca being in enemy hands, Abd-el-Malik, caliph of Damascus, decided to make El-Kuds the number one city. Because of this decision, he ordered the Dome of the Rock to be built.

At this time there were no Arab architects capable of fulfilling his wishes, and so like Solomon who had employed outsiders to help build the First Temple, the caliph employed Hellenized Syrians. These men produced a masterpiece. And today the Dome of the Rock is the best of that type of architecture in existence. The building has been carefully repaired from time to time, and in these repairs one can see the stamp of history—and human nature!

Hoping to add glory to his name, an imposter wrote in large letters in the inner arcade: "This Qubbat was built by the servant of Allah, Abdullah al-Imam, The Prince of believers, al-Ma'moon, in the year 72 AH, may Allah accept this and be pleased with him. Amen." This inscription was written in Arabic over the erased name of the real

Jerusalem

planner of the building: Ad-el-Malik. Curiously the glory-seeker did not change the date, and thus his hypocrisy is clearly apparent.

"AH" means "After the Hegira"—Mohammed's flight from Mecca to Medina. This flight occurred on July 16, 622. The year one in the Moslem calendar starts on July 1 of that year.

The Moslems claim that there is a gold chest within this mosque which contains two of Mohammed's whiskers. Whether this is true or not, Mecca remains the number one city in the Moslem world and Jerusalem a mere number three. The number two spot goes to Medina.

During the Crusades when Jerusalem was occupied by the Crusaders, the Dome of the Rock was used as a Christian church building. A cross was placed on top of the dome and the big rock was covered with marble and fenced in. The fence was necessary because Christian pilgrims insisted in chipping the stone for souvenirs. These chips, it is said, were worth their weight in gold.

The cross remained on the dome for less than a century, for Jerusalem was retaken by Saladin in 1187. Today the Dome of the Rock is within the jurisdiction of Israel. Nevertheless, it is still under the direct control of the Moslems, and sometimes they will not allow tourists to enter it. The Dome of the Rock remains one of the most interesting buildings in the world. It overflows with mystery, romance, and even intrigue; and to trace all the tales associated with it—many given with a shrug and a smile—would require a dozen lifetimes.

CHAPTER 13

Nazareth

Having seen Jerusalem and Bethlehem, almost every tourist is eager to go north and visit Nazareth—the boyhood town of Jesus. But having looked around the city, many are vaguely disappointed.

The cave with its carpenter shop above where Jesus allegedly stayed with Mary and Joseph seems quite unreal, and one is also tempted to doubt the authenticity of the Church of the Annunciation. It is claimed that this building was erected over the home of Mary's parents, and that it was here Gabriel announced to the startled teenager that she would conceive a child by the Holy Ghost and that His name would be Jesus.

There are places in Nazareth, however, that seem very real. For example, there is Mary's Well, also called the Virgin's Fountain. During the boyhood of Jesus, this was the city's main water supply. And without doubt Mary frequently was in Jesus' memory when He spoke to the Samaritan woman about "a well of water springing up into everlasting life" (John 4:14).

The old city of Nazareth with its quaint carpenter shops, noisy children, flat roofs, green cypress trees, and low hills

Nazareth

has seemingly not changed since Jesus walked its dusty streets. Still, one has serious questions. The paved streets, numbered houses, overhead wires make a difference as do also the sputtering automobiles and the glass windows in the shops and homes. In addition, it is an Arab city with an Arab mayor. I am certain that if Joseph were suddenly resurrected, he would blink a few times before he recognized where he was.

But there is one thing that has not changed much across the centuries: and this is the general topography of the land. And in this topography there remains a vital and extremely important story.

An efficiency expert might wonder why Jesus was conceived in Nazareth if He, to fulfill prophecy, was to be born in Bethlehem. Today, the sixty-five air miles from Nazareth to Bethlehem seem insignificant; but as Mary, great with child, made the journey it was a long, long trip—a trip that took several torturous days. Had He been conceived in Bethlehem or even Jerusalem such a trip would have been quite unnecessary.

Undoubtedly God had many reasons, and perhaps one of them was that He wanted to confirm to the world that He delights in doing mysterious things. Both Bethlehem and Jerusalem are mentioned many times in the Old Testament; but search as one will from Genesis through Malachi, one will not find a single reference to Nazareth. Moreover, New Testament Nazareth had a scurrilous reputation. It was the kind of town that caused Roman soldiers to smirk if they had a day or two to spend there. And all of us remember the words of Nathanael who exclaimed: "Can there by any good thing come out of Nazareth?" (John 1:46).

Nazareth—now called en-Natzirah—is perched on a hill within a cup formed by surrounding hills. These hills shut off the main view. But by climbing the rim and looking south, the Plain of Esdraelon—also called the Valley of Jezreel—stretches out to the dim hills of Samaria.

These plains encompass at least twenty battlefields.

Nazareth

From them swirled the dust stirred by the chariots of Egypt, Assyria, and Babylon. It was here Deborah defeated the Canaanites; and it was here that Saul and his three sons fell in their battle with the Philistines.

A glance at a topographical map of Palestine shows that the Plain of Esdraelon nearly cuts the country from the west of the Jordon River to the Mediterranean into two sections. And from the rim south of Nazareth, one can almost see two eras.

To the south, toward Jerusalem, one sees the Old Testament era; and toward the north, one sees Nazareth, Galilee, and other places made famous in the New Testament era. In the *must* book, *In the Steps of the Master,* H. V. Morton says: "Everyone must feel how different are these two worlds. In the New Testament we seem to have emerged from a dark, fierce Eastern world into a clear light that is almost European. The center of the Old Testament world is rigid, exclusive Jerusalem; the center of the New Testament world is Galilee, a country crossed in the time of Christ by the great military roads from the north and by the ancient caravan routes from the east."

This contrast between "New Testament" Galilee and "Old Testament" Judea is made even more sharp when we realize that Nazareth is less than twenty miles from the ever-fresh Sea of Galilee, while Jerusalem is approximately the same distance from the ever-dead Dead Sea. But at the same time we must keep in mind that both sections are connected by the Jordan River!

Jesus was conceived in New Testament Nazareth, but He was born in Old Testament Bethlehem. He grew up in New Testament Nazareth and chose His disciples—with the exception of Judas—in New Testament Galilee. But He was crucified and resurrected in Old Testament Jerusalem.

Also, Jesus preached in Old Testament Jerusalem, but most of His ministry was in New Testament Galilee. The two sections, in many ways, were separate, and yet in other ways they were combined. Was all of this planned by

Nazareth

Visitors to Nazareth today see a city of contrasts as they view beautiful memorial stained glass windows in a modern church commemorating the home of Joseph and Mary and saunter down ancient cobblestone streets where the gutter for refuse runs down the middle.

Nazareth

God, or are we reading something into the map and history that is not intended? It is an intriguing question. But here are some facts.

After Joseph and Mary had fled to Egypt because of their fear of Herod, they learned that Herod was dead. They then decided to return to Judea. "But when he [Joseph] heard that Archelaus did reign in Judea in the room of his father Herod, he was afraid to go thither ... he turned aside into the parts of Galilee. And he came and dwelt in a city called Nazareth: that it might be fulfilled which was spoken by the prophets, He shall be called a Nazarene" (Matthew 2: 22, 23).

Following His temptation near Jericho in Judea, Jesus returned to Nazareth. And there "he went into the synagogue on the sabbath day, and stood up for to read. And there was delivered unto him the book of the prophet Esaias. And when he had opened the book, he found the place where it was written, The Spirit of the Lord is upon me, because he hath anointed me to preach the gospel to the poor; he hath sent me to heal the brokenhearted, to preach deliverance to the captives, and recovering of sight to the blind, to set at liberty them that are bruised, To preach the acceptable year of the Lord" (Luke 4:16-19).

After Jesus had finished reading, he closed the book, handed it to the minister and said: "This day is this scripture fulfilled in your ears" (verse 21).

Angry because of what Jesus had claimed, they rose up "and thrust him out of the city, and led him unto the brow of the hill whereon their city was built, that they might cast him down headlong. But he passing through the midst of them went his way" (Luke 4:29, 30).

Today, this place where they wanted to throw Jesus from the cliff is known as the Hill of Precipitation. Some of this hill is disappearing, for the Israelis are quarrying rock from it to be used in building projects.

But in spite of this rejection, Jesus remained for a time in Galilee. From Nazareth He went to Capernaum, "a city of Galilee," and there He began to assemble the Twelve. The

Nazareth

Another street of the boyhood town of Jesus favors the tourist trade where unique items of the Eastern culture can be found. Nazareth today is mainly an Arab city and boasts many modern apartment buildings.

Nazareth

debate will never be settled, but there are some who feel that Jesus was rejected from Nazareth a second time. The second occasion is recorded in Matthew 13:54.

After each of these incidents—assuming that there were two—Jesus said: "A prophet is not without honour, save in his own country, and in his own house" (Matthew 13:57). But although the saying is true, he never forgot Nazareth!

The dramatic connection between Nazareth and Jerusalem had an unusual exposure in 1878. At that time, a slab of marble with an inscription on it, found in Nazareth, was sent to a German collector of antiquarian items. Froehner, the collector, apparently saw nothing unusual about the inscription. But after it was given to the Louvre in 1930, a noted historian, Michel Medailles, was startled by what he read and published his findings in 1932.

The inscription, according to his translation, says: "Ordinance of Caesar. It is my pleasure that graves and tombs remain undisturbed in perpetuity for those who have made them for the cult of their ancestors, or children or members of their house. If, however, any man lay information that another has either demolished them, or has in any other way extracted the buried, or has maliciously transferred them to other places in order to wrong them, or had displaced the sealing or other stones, against such a one I order that a trial be instituted, as in respect of the gods, so in regard to the cult of mortals. For it shall be much more obligatory to honor the buried. Let it be absolutely forbidden for anyone to disturb them. In the case of contravention I desire that the offender be sentenced to capital punishment on the charge of violation of sepulture."

Scholars believe that this law was made by the Roman Emperor Claudius around A.D. 50. It was a year before this that Claudius expelled the Jews from Rome (Acts 18:2). The exciting thing about the find is that it tends to support the belief in the resurrection of Jesus Christ. Claudius, though considered a fool by many, was an accomplished scholar—and his writings fill many a

Nazareth

volume. He was angry at the Jews, and according to Suetonius, "the Jews at Rome caused continuous disturbances at the instigation of Chrestus." Because of this "he expelled them from the city."

Could it be that Claudius was convinced that the Jews were especially energetic because of their belief in the Resurrection? Yes, that is entirely possible. And this belief may have inspired his edict. Perhaps he was afraid there might be another "contrived" resurrection. But why was the slab found in Nazareth, when Jesus was resurrected in Jerusalem?

Once again, no one knows. But in God's plan, Nazareth and Jerusalem have a mysterious connection, just as the Old and the New Testaments have a mysterious connection.

Selected Bibliography

A great deal of information is available on the subject of cities which formed the background of the life and activities of the people of New Testament times. The following books have been especially useful in the preparation of this book and are recommended for the general reader.

Downey, Glanville, *Ancient Antioch*. Princeton, N.J.: Princeton University Press, 1963.

Durant, Will, *Caesar and Christ*. New York: Simon and Schuster, 1944.

Elton, Lord, *Gordon of Khartoum*. New York: Alfred A. Knopf, Inc., 1954.

Gibbon, Edward, *The Decline and Fall of the Roman Empire*. New York: E. P. Dutton & Co.

Hamblin, Dora Jane and Crunsfeld, Mary Jane, *The Appian Way. A Journey*. New York: Random House, 1974.

Juvenal, *Satire*.

Kenyon, Kathleen M., *Digging Up Jericho*. New York: Frederick A. Praeger, 1957.

Morton, H. V., *In the Steps of St. Paul*. London: Rich & Cowan, Ltd.

Paoli, Ugo, *Rome—Its People, Life and Customs*. David McCoy, Inc. Copyright, Longmans Green, 1963.

Ramsey, William M., *St. Paul the Traveller and the Roman Citizen*. Grand Rapids: Baker Book House, reprint.

Suetonius, *The Twelve Caesars*. New York: Penguin Books. Copyright by Robert Graves.

Wood, J. T., Modern Discoveries on the Site of Ancient Ephesus. The Religious Tract Society, 1890.

Xenophon, *Anabasis,* I.11.20. The Loeb Classical Library, Translated by Carleton L. Brownson.